ISBN 978-1-331-95344-9
PIBN 10259010

This book is a reproduction of an important historical work. Forgotten Books uses
state-of-the-art technology to digitally reconstruct the work, preserving the original format
whilst repairing imperfections present in the aged copy. In rare cases, an imperfection in
the original, such as a blemish or missing page, may be replicated in our edition. We do,
however, repair the vast majority of imperfections successfully; any imperfections that
remain are intentionally left to preserve the state of such historical works.

1 MONTH OF
FREE
READING

at
www.ForgottenBooks.com

By purchasing this book you are eligible for one month membership to ForgottenBooks.com, giving you unlimited access to our entire collection of over 700,000 titles via our web site and mobile apps.

To claim your free month visit:

www.forgottenbooks.com/free259010

English
Français
Deutsche
Italiano
Español
Português

www.forgottenbooks.com

Mythology Photography **Fiction**
Fishing Christianity **Art** Cooking
Essays Buddhism Freemasonry
Medicine **Biology** Music **Ancient
Egypt** Evolution Carpentry Physics
Dance Geology **Mathematics** Fitness
Shakespeare **Folklore** Yoga Marketing
Confidence Immortality Biographies
Poetry **Psychology** Witchcraft
Electronics Chemistry History **Law**
Accounting **Philosophy** Anthropology
Alchemy Drama Quantum Mechanics
Atheism Sexual Health **Ancient History**
Entrepreneurship Languages Sport
Paleontology Needlework Islam
Metaphysics Investment Archaeology
Parenting Statistics Criminology
Motivational

HISTORICAL ADDRESS

DELIVERED AT THE

CENTENNIAL CELEBRATION,

IN

Easthampton, Mass.,

JULY 4, 1876.

By REV. PAYSON W. LYMAN.

SPRINGFIELD, MASS.:
THE CLARK W. BRYAN COMPANY, PRINTERS.
1877.

HISTORICAL ADDRESS

DELIVERED AT THE

CENTENNIAL CELEBRATION,

IN

Easthampton, Mass.,

JULY 4, 1876.

By REV. PAYSON W. LYMAN.

SPRINGFIELD, MASS.:

CLARK W. BRYAN & COMPANY, PRINTERS.

1877.

INTRODUCTORY.

—•••—

A MEETING of the citizens interested in having a celebration, with an historical address, on the Centennial 4th of July, was held at the Mansion House on the 'evening of June 21, 1876.

Lieutenant-Governor Knight was called to the chair.

After a free and full interchange of views, it was voted to appoint a committee of five to consider the matter, and report at a subsequent meeting.

The committee consisted of Lieut-Governor H. G. KNIGHT, Hon. E. H. SAWYER, Dea. LAUREN D. LYMAN, Dea. C. B. JOHNSON, OSCAR WARD.

The committee subsequently reported that it is expedient to have a celebration, with an historical address, whereupon it was

Voted, To invite the Rev. Payson W. Lyman of Belchertown, to deliver the address, and C. B. Johnson was appointed a committee to ascertain if Mr. Lyman would accept the invitation. He subsequently reported that Mr. Lyman had consented to deliver the address.

It was also voted, that E. R. Bosworth and John Mayher be appointed a committee on finance.

Subsequent meetings, in furtherance of the object, were held as follows: One on the evening of June 22d, another on the evening of the 24th, and still another on the evening of the 26th. The final meeting was held June 30th.

At these meetings it was

Voted, That the preliminary Committee of Five be a permanent Committee of Arrangements.

Voted, That Maj. Henry E. Alvord be appointed chief marshal, with power to employ as many assistants as he may require.

Voted, To appoint Henry H. Sawyer a committee on vocal music.

Voted, To invite all the Sabbath-schools in the town to unite in the celebration, and the invitation was accepted.

Voted, That the address be delivered in the town hall, and that the exercises begin at 3 o'clock P. M.

Voted, That James Keene, superintendent of the Sabbath-school in the First church, A. J. Lyman, superintendent of the school in the Payson church, S. W. Pierce, superintendent of the Methodist Sabbath-school, N. W. Farrar, superintendent of the school in the Episcopal Society, and the Rev. R. J. Donovan, of the Catholic Sabbath-school, be requested to make the necessary arrangements for their respective schools. It was decided to set the tables for refreshments in the Seminary grounds.

Voted, That the Easthampton Cornet Band be engaged to furnish music for the procession.

The One Hundredth Anniversary of our National Independence was ushered in by the ringing of bells, firing of cannon, blazing of bonfires, and other demonstrations of joy; and a procession, headed by a drum corps, marching through the principal streets, in the early gray of the morning, finished the first act. At 9 o'clock, A. M., the Manhan Hose company, in full uniform, headed by the Easthampton Cornet Band, paraded the streets, making an imposing appearance. There has been no demonstration like it in the town for many years.

At 3 o'clock in the afternoon, the exercises in the town hall were opened by Hon. E. H. Sawyer, in behalf of the Committee of Arrangements, who spoke as follows:

One hundred years ago to-day, our fathers, few in number, but strong in faith and hope, declared themselves free and independent, and capable of self-government. From that day to this, they and their descendants have maintained the truth of that declaration; and this afternoon, in our established freedom, we have gathered in this place to speak of the good way the Lord has led us in the hundred years just past. After the manner set us by our forefathers, to secure an orderly meeting, a Committee of Arrangements, chosen for the purpose at a preliminary gathering, have agreed to propose officers for this occasion; and as directed by said committee, I now nominate as president of the day, our townsman, native-born, His Honor the Lieutenant-Governor of this Commonwealth; and as secretaries, Lafayette Clapp, Esq., and C. B. Johnson, Esq.

The nominations were carried unanimously, and Governor Knight, on taking the chair, spoke as follows:

I cheerfully and gratefully take the place assigned to me on this occasion by the Committee of Arrangements; cheerfully, because the duties of the position will be easily performed; and gratefully, because it is an honorable one, and my call to it furnishes evidence of the continued good-will of my associates and fellow-citizens, whose uniform and abounding kindness has placed me under the greatest obligations.

In accordance with the proclamation of the chief magistrate of the nation, it is becoming in us, as a Christian people, on this one hundredth birthday of our republic, to assemble, as we have done; render thanks to God for his goodness to us in the century that has passed; for our freedom and union; for our arts and industries; for our fields and factories; for our trade and commerce; for our homes, our schools, and churches; and for all his benefits to us as a nation; and to beseech Him that he will be our guide and defence during all the years of the century upon which we are now entering.

It will not be proper for me to occupy the time that has been assigned to others, and thus detain you from the feast that has been prepared. The scenes of this day forcibly remind me of the great changes that have come over our own little town during the last few years. Some of us remember when our population was only about one-sixth of what it is to-day, and when the noble families of Clarks, Clapps, Lymans and Wrights, constituted a majority. We also had a goodly though smaller number of Pomeroys.

Our attention is soon to be directed to some facts and events in our local history, by one of the Lyman family, whose tastes and studies have well fitted him for the service. As we listen to his words, may we remember, and never forget, that a pure and upright character is the most precious relic of our past history which we can cherish; and that such a character, built up in us and our children, is the noblest monument we can erect to the memory of our fathers, and of the men who laid the foundations of our government. I am not among those who think the former times were greatly better than the present, and who take a desponding view of the future. We have seen some decay of private virtue and public honor; but now we witness a quickened spirit of honor and integrity in the management of public affairs, a growing contempt for dishonesty and dishonest men, and a hatred of every form of fraud and falsehood, which may well lead us to thank God and take courage.

Permit me to express the earnest hope, that by the exercises of this hour, and by all the grateful and patriotic memories of the day, we may be inspired with new thankfulness to the God who upheld our fathers in their struggle for liberty and independence; and who has carried their children through the trials of the century; and that we may all make vows of new devotion to the unity and welfare of our dear country, and the preservation and purity of its institutions.

, Representative Lafayette Clapp then read the President's proclamation, after which prayer was offered by Rev. A. M. Colton, the audience joining in the Lord's Prayer at the end. Next, the Star Spangled Banner was sung by a select choir, under the direction of H. H. Sawyer. The Declaration of Independence was read by Capt. David Hill, and after the singing of Keller's National Hymn, the Rev. Payson Williston Lyman, of Belchertown, was announced as the speaker of the day.

At the close of the address, William G. Bassett, Esq., offered the following resolution, which was unanimously adopted :

Resolved, That the thanks of the meeting be returned to Rev. Payson W. Lyman, for his appropriate and entertaining address; and that a copy be requested of him, to the end that the Committee of Arrangements may comply with President Grant's proclamation, relating to the preservation of historical addresses.

The audience then joined in singing America; Rev. Dr. S. T. Seelye followed with a few remarks, and closed the exercises in the hall with the benediction.

One prominent and very interesting feature of the occasion was, that the platform was filled with a large number of the elderly men of the town.

After the close of the exercises in the hall, the Sabbath-schools were formed in procession, under the direction of Chief-Marshal Alvord, and after marching through the streets for a while, brought up in the Seminary grounds, in front of the well filled tables; and proceeded to perform the part of the programme assigned to them, in a manner satisfactory to themselves, and equally so to their friends.

The fire-works in the evening, owing to signs of rain, began a full hour earlier than was expected, and many of the best pieces were lost to the crowd. A slight shower coming up about that time, the large concourse gathered sought their homes, being a little disappointed, perhaps, at this part of the day's proceedings, but, on the whole, well satisfied with the celebration of the Centennial Fourth.

Historical Address.

———•••———

Two hundred and eleven years ago, December 13, 1664, the town of Northampton granted John Webb a piece of land "at Pascommuck," to build a house upon. The house he is supposed to have built the following Spring; and it was the first civilized habitation within the borders of our town. It stood near the residence of the late Augustus Clapp, in Nashawannuck. It was on a little rise of ground, near the bank of the river, at the westernmost bend of the "old bed," which was then the only channel. This was ten years after the actual settlement of Northampton, in 1654.

The purchase of the tract of land known as Nonotuck, from the aboriginal owners thereof, was made in 1653. Upon May 6th of that year, certain inhabitants of Windsor, Hartford and other places, twenty-four in number, petitioned the General Court for liberty "to plant, possess and inhabit the place, being on the Conetiquot river, above Springfield, called Nonotuck." They represented that they knew the place to be "desirable to erect a town in, for the furtherance of the public weal, by providing corn and raising cattle, not only for their own, but likewise for the good of others—the propagating of the Gospel—the place promising, in an ordinary way of God's providence, a comfortable subsistence, whereby people may live, and attend upon God in his holy ordinances without distraction." This petition was aided by three of the principal men of Springfield, John Pyncheon, Elizur Holyoke, and Samuel Chapin, who, upon the granting of the petition, May 18, 1653, were appointed commissioners to lay out Nonotuck into two plantations, of which the petitioners were to have one. The other, subsequently laid out, was east of the river.

The first public document on record in Northampton, in the words "not molesting Indians, nor depriving them of their just rights and property, without allowance to their satisfaction," recognizes the principle upon which our fathers proceeded in effecting settlement. Accordingly, September 24, 1653, their representative, John Pyncheon, effected a purchase of this region, at Springfield. Conveyance of title was made by six prominent Indians, sachems of the Norwottuck tribe and others, two of whom appear as owners of land east of the river.

The tract of land purchased, according to Sylvester Judd's version of the deed, *" Extended from the brook below Munhan, called Shankwonk, below Asahel Lyman's," (i e. the brook crossing the highway, not far above Smith's ferry,) " up by the Quinetticott, to the brook or gutter below Capawonk, called Masquomp, (now Half-way brook,) and out into the woods westerly nine miles." Hoyt and others make it to have extended downward to the Falls on the Connecticut at South Hadley. The price paid was 100 fathom of wampum, 10 coats, and the plowing of 16 acres of land

*History of Hadley, page 114.

on the east side of the river. A fathom of wampum, of white beads, was worth five shillings, and of black beads ten shillings.

The settlement was effected the following Spring, though only a third of the original petitioners are thought to have become actual settlers. One of these was John Webb, who, ten years after, made the first settlement within the present limits of East-hampton.

July 20, 1657, the settlers bought the South meadow in Hatfield, called by the Indians Capawonk, of Sachem Umpanchala, otherwise Womscom or Lampanobo, for fifty shillings, which was received from "John Webb of Northampton," who no doubt acted as the town's agent.

Being desirous of encouraging a settlement higher up the river, between them and the northern wilderness,—a motive which had actuated Springfield in favoring our settlement—they sold this tract the next year, October 17, 1658, to certain Hartford men who proposed to settle across the river from Northampton, for £10, to be paid in wheat and peas. They stipulated, among other things, that settlement should be begun by May, 1659, and that they should settle on both sides of the river. Some of the conditions of sale were not complied with, and March 11, 1659, we find John Webb and two others, in behalf of Northampton, agreeing with three representatives of the new plantation, to sell Capawonk meadow for £30 sterling, to be paid in wheat and peas delivered in Hartford. This agreement is the first instrument recorded in the book of deeds in Springfield. The deed, for some reason, was not given till January 22, 1663.

These new settlers bought of the Indians the land stretching nine miles east of the river, and extending from Mount Holyoke to Mount Toby. Also, at a later date, a tract lying along the west bank of the river, above Capawonk, running back nine miles. Pyncheon, who, with Holyoke and Chapin of Springfield, and William Holton and Richard Lyman of Northampton, was appointed to lay out the new plantation, negotiated these purchases, as he was an influential man and a great trader. This second settlement in old Nonotuck was at first called Newtown or Norwottuck; but at its incorporation, May 22, 1661, it took the name Hadley.

These accounts of the purchase of Indian lands make it clear that our fathers did no injustice to the natives. It is said that they welcomed the English, and gladly sold their lands, knowing well to what use the English were accustomed to put them. Though the price received was small, it was all they demanded, and all the lands were worth, considering the hardships, risks and costs to be endured, in effecting settlement in a wilderness, and reducing the land to cultivation. And then the Indians, in reality, surrendered little which was of value to themselves. It was understood that they might still dwell, hunt, and fish, within the territory sold. Two of the deeds expressly permit them to set up their wigwams and get fire-wood from the commons. They had little use for the land for other purposes than these. " It may well be doubted," says Sylvester Judd, " whether all the Indian corn fields in the valley, from Holyoke and Tom on the south, to Toby and Sugar Loaf on the north, contained more than seventy acres." In Hadley one corn field of sixteen acres, more or less, was expressly exempted from sale. They lost little, therefore, for the men continued to hunt and fish, and the women to raise corn, perhaps even to better advantage, upon shares, on well plowed lands, than ever before "It would be difficult, perhaps," says Mr. Judd, "to tell why the purchase of Indian lands in Pennsylvania, by William Pènn, is more worthy of renown than the purchase of Indian lands in Northampton and Hadley, by John Pyncheon, twenty years before." The principal chiefs of the Norwottucks, north of Mounts Tom and Hòlyoke, at the period of settlement, were Chickwallop, Umpanchala and Quonquont, whose names are prominent in the early deeds.

The first white resident within the limits of Easthampton, as has been shown, was John Webb, who seems to have been an honored citizen of our mother town. His land was granted December 13, 1664, and settlement made, probably, in the ensuing Spring. At what time he died is uncertain. Robert Danks, an early resident of Northampton, married his widow, and, with two sons of Webb, lived in Nashawannuck many years. Descendants of Webb were there for seventy-five years.

The first bridge over the Manhan river was voted in 1668, and most likely was near the house of John Webb, and not far from where the meadow road now crosses the same stream. Over this the settlers conveyed such of their produce as they did not require for home consumption. Their taxes were payable first at Charlestown, and afterwards at Boston, in wheat. This was conveyed to Hartford in carts and wagons, and thence shipped to Boston. The cost of shipping from Hartford, in at least one recorded instance, consumed one-third of the cargo.

Just across the Manhan from the homestead of John Webb, at the foot of the mountain, is a beautiful plateau, overlooking the meadows, and Northampton beyond. It is at the point where now the road leading up the mountain which bears up the ancient name of this section,—Nonotuck—takes its departure from the public highway. This was the location of the next residences within our limits, and the hamlet planted here bore the Indian name Pascommuck. The settlers were five in number, Moses Hutchinson, John Searle, Benoni Jones, Samuel and Benjamin Janes, with their families. The town granted them their home lots in 1699.

They were not, however, destined to remain long in undisturbed possession of their homes. On the 24th of May, 1704, early in the morning, a party of non-resident Indians, passing this way, came down from the mountain and fell upon the hamlet so suddenly, and so impetuously, that defence, though attempted, was impossible. Nineteen persons, nine of the name of Janes, were slain, either here, or shortly after capture. Benjamin Janes escaped from his captors, and, rowing to Northampton across the flooded meadows, gave the alarm. A troop of cavalry, under Capt. John Taylor, speedily started in pursuit, who encountered the Indians, but with no other result than the death of nearly all the captives, and of Captain Taylor himself. Another troop afterwards came up from the lower settlements to punish the savages, but were unsuccessful. More than ten years elapsed before this ruin was repaired, but at length other persons came in to take the places of the slain, some of them being children of the slain.

Twenty-five years before the settlement at Pascommuck, or in 1674, Northampton gave "David Wilton, Medad Pumry, and Joseph Taylor, liberty to erect a saw-mill on the brook, on the right hand of the cart-way going over Manhan river." Twelve years later, (1686-7) they voted Samuel Bartlett liberty to set up a corn-mill, "on the falls below the cart-way on the river." The cart-way was just above our covered bridge at the foot of Meeting House hill. These mills were doubtless built soon after, though their owners did not effect a residence here. Samuel Bartlett gave the corn-mill to his son Joseph in 1705, who made the first permanent settlement in the region of the present village, probably as early as 1725 or 30. His house he kept open for the accommodation of travelers for twenty years. His nephew, Jonathan Clapp, ancestor of all the Clapps among us, lived with him and succeeded to the greater portion of his estate, and to his business. About the same time at which Landlord Joseph Bartlett built his house, his brother David settled some forty rods westerly from the present residence of Julius Pomeroy, and after him his son lived there till near or quite the time of the Revolution. Between the homes of the Bartlett brothers was the home of four brothers named Wait, not far from where R. C. Dresser now lives.

Twenty years later, May 28, 1745, Deacon Stephen Wright and Benjamin Lyman, bought of Northampton the upper School meadow, a tract of eighty acres of land, lying on both sides of the river above the cart-way, which the town had set apart for the support of schools.* Deacon Wright settled where Samuel Hurlburt lives, and Mr. Lyman where Joel Bassett lives. They were the ancestors of the Wrights and

---

* The original deed may be seen in the museum.

Lymans of Easthampton, and, until recently, most of their lands have been held by descendants.

Not far from 1732, Samuel and Eldad Pomeroy, settled upon what is now the homestead of Dea. E. W. Hannum and son. Caleb, son of Samuel, soon after built near the late residence of A. L. Strong. In 1742, the Pomeroys entered a protest to the General Court, against being set off from Northampton with the then recent settlers in what is now Southampton, who were moving for separation, and with whom they had had no connection. In their address, they state that they had improved their lands, and paid taxes upon them for forty or fifty years. This would seem to show that their land came under cultivation not later than 1700. They were, afterwards, at their own request, received into the new society at Southampton.

As early as 1750, Josiah Phelps established himself upon Park hill, upon the place, until lately, for many years occupied by J. Rockwell Wright. About 1760 John and Eleazer Hannum settled upon the plateau now occupied by J. Milton and Edwin Hannum.

The first settler upon the plain upon which our village stands, was Serg. Ebenezer Corse, who built a house where Spencer Clapp formerly lived, and cut his road for a mile through the forest to this point. He was followed soon after by Stephen Wright, Jr., and Benjamin Lyman, Jr., sons of the purchasers of School meadow, and also by Benjamin and Aaron Clapp, the posterity of all of whom, John and Luther L. Wright, Ansel B. Lyman, William N. Clapp and son, and James H. Lyman, still occupy their ancestral seats. The first settlement in the south-east part of the town was effected by Israel Hendrick, about a hundred years since.

The first settlers of Southampton were mostly from Northampton, sons of men with large families, who wished to find homes for their children. The first meeting of those proposing to effect a settlement there, of which there is any record, was held January 31, 1730. A committee of Northampton citizens divided the lands among them. The first recorded notice of this settlement, afterwards called "the second precinct," was in the account of a meeting held December 22, 1732, when a committee was chosen "to lay out a highway, over the branch of Manhan river, at or near Pomeroy's meadow, or some other suitable and convenient place, so as to accommodate the new settlement." In 1732, two houses were erected there, and in 1733, fourteen; and shortly after fourteen more. This, in brief, was the origin of Southampton. It was established by the General Court as the second precinct of Northampton, July 23, 1741, on petition of thirty-five freeholders, one of whom was Eleazer Hannum of our town. They had preaching from the first, whenever they could secure it. In 1737, measures were taken to secure a house of worship, which was begun but not completed for several years. The first pastor, Rev. Jonathan Judd, was ordained June 8, 1743. Serg. Ebenezer Corse, before mentioned, was the only one who voted against Mr. Judd's settlement, and he afterwards became a decided supporter of the new minister. In 1753, they appointed a committee "to dignify the seats and pews." The relative dignity of citizens was determined by a combination of age and property, one year in age being equal to £10 in property.

2

For more than a century after Webb's settlement
in Nashawannuck, those who resided within our borders had their civil and ecclesiastical relations with
North or Southampton.   They shared with those
towns the perils of Indian hostilities; they joined
with them in the support of the Gospel.   Side by
side they marched with British soldiers in the early
French and Indian wars.   They endured toil and pri-
vation, and some of them shed their blood, on the
fields about Lake George, Louisburg and elsewhere.
The names of those soldiers are mostly forgotten, and
the record of their individual service, saving in ex-
ceptional cases, has perished.   But their heroism and
valor helped to procure this country for the use of an
English speaking and liberty loving race.   Along
with the heroes of later wars, they should be awarded
honored places in the regard of those who, in this
and succeeding generations, enjoy the priceless herit-
age won by their valor.

Excepting the massacre already referred to at Pascommuck, no record has come to us of the death of
any one, at the hands of the Indians, within our borders, excepting Nathaniel Edwards of Northampton,
who was shot and scalped in 1724, near the brook
which crosses the highway, just south of the residence
of Samuel Phelps.

Long before this, the Norwottuck Indians, of whom
the lands were bought, had ceased to make Nonotuck
their home.   For twenty years after their sale of the
lands, they dwelt here, in perfect peace with the settlers.

In 1664, they were allowed to build a fort upon
certain conditions, such as that they should not harbor hostile Indians, nor violate the Sabbath by bear-

ing burdens upon it. This fort was probably the one
on Fort hill, near its north-east point, overlooking the
meadows, east of the present South street in Northampton. Mr. Judd says that the forts of the Norwottucks were generally built upon a bluff, or high bank,
projecting into a valley or intervale, near a stream.
They also had a fort on Fort plain, the plateau in the
rear of our East street school-house, overlooking the
meadows of the Manhan and Connecticut. Here was
the last residence of Indians within the limits of Easthampton. Their last place of habitation within Nonotuck was on another Fort plain, about half way from
Northampton to Hatfield, where they had a fort on
the high bank of the Connecticut, overlooking Hadley Great meadow.

In 1675, they showed evident signs of hostility.
This disposition was so marked, that the settlers determined to disarm them, peaceably if possible, but to
disarm them at all events. Their negotiations failed,
and they planned a surprise for the night succeeding
August 24, 1675. But the Indians, anticipating the
attempt, had fled, having killed an old sachem who
would not go. Pursuit of them resulted in an encounter, in which our troops lost nine men. One of
the Indian women afterwards claimed that they lost
twenty-six, though Mr. Judd doubts so large a loss.
At all events, they retired up the valley and never
returned to dwell. One, at least, of their women was
friendly to the last, and warned " goodwife Wright "
to get into the town with her children, and said she
dared not to tell the news, for her tribe would then
cut off her head. No doubt some of them, the women
especially, left their ancestral home in fair Nonotuck
with heavy hearts. Mr. Judd estimates that, at this

time, this clan or tribe numbered two hundred or more.

During this period the people were necessarily on the watch against the forces of Philip, and maintained, during the war, a permanent guard, which, in 1676, two hundred years ago, numbered fifty. In the famous Turners Falls fight, in which our forces were under command of Captain Turner, and in which a decisive blow was struck against Philip, our Northampton soldiers were under command of Ensign John Lyman ; and rendered efficient service.

But though no Indians resided in Nonotuck after the close of Philip's war, yet there were periods when the people were, with good reason, seriously apprehensive of an attack ; and when families lay down at night not knowing what horror would befall them before the dawn ; when in going to the field or town a weapon of war was a necessary appurtenance ; and when the mother, at home with the children, felt the need of vigilant watch against a surprise. Especially does this appear to have been the case in the years 1745-6-7; for at this time watch houses were built, and a dwelling in each hamlet fortified. The houses of Joseph Bartlett at the mills, Samuel Janes at Pascommuck, and Maj. Jonathan Clapp on the Northampton road, were thus fortified.

During all these years, the population of this region was enlarging ; new homesteads were being brought under cultivation ; and the people were establishing a center for themselves. Occasional preaching services were enjoyed at the house of Landlord Bartlett ; and they at length felt that their numbers and property would warrant a separate town and church organization. Accordingly, in March, 1773, they began to press the matter of separation, representing their desire that they might be in such circumstances, that, with little difficulty, they could meet and transact business among themselves; but more especially that with greater convenience, and hopefully, with greater profit to themselves and their families, they might attend on public worship, and on the ordinances of God's sanctuary. The religious motive was thus uppermost in the minds of our fathers in seeking to build a new township.

Northampton acquiesced in their request; voted them £300 for religious uses; and directed its representative in General Court to forward their petition. But the strenuous opposition of Southampton postponed the final act till after the Revolution. Again in 1781-2, the matter was agitated, and a Northampton committee reported that "the petitioners with their lands, together with those from Southampton who wished to join them, would make a respectable parish or town, and be fully sufficient to support the charges incident thereto." They recommended that their petition be granted, and the town adopted the recommendation, voting to give the new town one-eighth the public lands and other property. The act of incorporation as a district was not granted till 1785.

The first district meeting was held at the house of Capt. Joseph Clapp, which house is still standing, just north of the covered bridge. The warrant was directed to Benjamin Lyman as "one of the principal inhabitants," and he was moderator of the meeting, which chose Dea. Stephen Wright, Capt. Philip Clark, and Eleazer Hannum, selectmen.

Before this time, in anticipation of incorporation,

certain individuals made preparation to build a house of worship; and, in the Spring of 1785, a frame was erected. At the first business meeting of the district, true to their declared religious purpose, the citizens voted to provide a place of worship, taking for that purpose the frame already erected, and paying its owners for the same.

November 17, 1785, the first church was organized, also at the house of Capt. Joseph Clapp. The membership of the church was seventy-two, of whom forty-six were from the church in Northampton, and twenty-six from that in Southampton.

Of this meeting Stephen Wright was moderator, and Capt. Philip Clark clerk, who, with Benjamin Lyman, were chosen deacons. Captain Clark declined filling this office, and two years later Obadiah Janes was chosen to it. Revs. Solomon Williams and Jonathan Judd, from whose churches the members of the new church had come, were present at the organization, as were Revs. Joseph Strong and Enoch Hale.

April 6, 1789, the church called Rev. Payson Williston to become their pastor. Accepting the call, he was ordained August 13th, the sermon upon the occasion being preached by Rev. Noah Williston, and the consecrating prayer being offered by Rev. Richard S. Storrs.

That ordination was an event heavily freighted with the future of the town. It gave us the man who was the people's religious teacher for forty-four years, and their revered and honored father for twenty more. In his loins as yet, but there on that day, by anticipation, was also the man who gave Easthampton its manufacturing industries, and its distinguished position as an educational center. That

day gave Williston, with all that that honored name
involves, to Easthampton. It was a great day for
Easthampton, was it not? August 13, 1789.

At the time of its organization the town is said to
have contained about sixty-five families; in all, some
four hundred inhabitants. The population in 1790
was four hundred and fifty-seven.

Thus, in outline, I have sketched the beginnings of
our goodly town; its actual beginnings in settlement,
together with the antecedent settlement of the
mother town; its municipal beginnings in incorporation; its ecclesiastical beginnings in church organization. If you would know its territorial beginnings,
you must ask the geologist, who, from the rocks,
and the soils, and the configuration of the region,
has read something of the physical history of these
stately ranges, and smiling slopes, and beauteous
intervales. The result of the conflicts and strug-
gles of nature's mighty forces, forms the basis of
that which, having been garnished by man's indus-
trious hand, constitutes as fair a landscape as any on
which the eye can rest.

But I must hasten to speak of that which is more
germane to this day, the war of the Revolution and
the part our fathers played.

THE WAR OF THE REVOLUTION,

In its inception and early intention, was not a war
for the acquisition of new privileges, but simply for
the maintenance of the old and time honored. Although nominally colonists of Great Britain, our people, from the beginning, had enjoyed, almost completely, the benefits of home rule. They had scarcely
been compelled to feel the power of the mother gov-

ernment at all. By what Burke calls "the wise neglect" of Great Britain, we had been left to the government of our own affairs. The people spoke their minds in the town meetings, and sent their representatives to General Court to record their will, and to bring it into harmony with the will of their sister townships. The towns managed their own ecclesiastical, educational, and military affairs; took part in the execution of justice through the local police and jurors whom they chose; levied taxes for these and other purposes; and discussed, in open meeting, questions relating to matters of public interest. The records of these town meetings are full of interest, and go far to show where the spirit of patriotism was fired to the requisite point. They are, indeed, the wonder and admiration of students of political philosophy, everywhere.

In matters of public as well as of municipal interest, the people were their own masters. The representative bodies which they elected appointed the governor's council, and directed our militia, judicial, and revenue system. No tax had ever been levied upon us by imperial authority. The people themselves, had thus become trained to self government, to which they had shown themselves entirely competent.

Now the so-called Revolution, in its beginning, was the people's determination to maintain possession of this inheritance which they had received from their ancestors, and to perpetuate the system which had been in force for a century and more. They were, in short, not innovators, but conservators.

The growth and prosperity of the colonies, however, excited the jealousy of the mother country; and a system of taxation was resolved upon, in order that the colonies might become a direct source of revenue.

In 1765, the odious Stamp Act was passed; but was resisted by our people so strenuously, that it was repealed. Parliament, however, nullified the effect of the repeal, by reasserting the principle that they had a right, both to tax the colonies, and to legislate for them in all cases whatever. This assertion alarmed the colonies, and put them in the attitude of resistance. For they held dear the right of legislation for themselves; and our own Major Hawley but voiced the public sentiment, when he openly declared in General Court, " that he knew not how Parliament could ever have acquired a right to legislate over the colonies." Then came the tea tax, which the people everywhere met by the resolve to drink no tea.

The oppressive Boston Port Bill, which followed, was met by the "solemn league and covenant" to use no English goods during the continuance of the blockade; a resolution which other open ports patriotically shared. It was requested that all the people of the province should unite in this resolution to use no imported goods. Governor Gage issued a proclamation forbidding the people to subscribe to the agreement; and threatening, if they did so, to transport them to England to be tried for treason. An entry in the Belchertown records of this period, is of interest, as showing the effect of the threat upon the people of this region. Chose ten men " to inspect the town, and see that there is not any goods exposed to sale in Belchertown, that were imported after the 1st day of December last."

After the Port Bill came the Restraining Acts, the design of which was to exclude us from the coast fish-

eries.   The royal Governors, Bernard, Hutchinson, and
Gage, had proceeded on the assumption that the legislature of Massachusetts must act in entire subordination to the administration in England; and the evident determination of Gage to insist upon it, intensi-
fied the popular discontent.   The military occupation
of the province, one incident of which had been the
Boston Massacre, increased the alarm.

But the measures which, of all others, if successful, would have been fatal to home rule, and the destruction of the inherited popular liberty, were what
are known as the "Regulation Acts of 1774."   These
ordained that the governor's council, as well as himself, should be chosen by the king, who also was to
hold in his hands the superior judges.   Furthermore
the inferior judges, and the sheriffs, were made de-
pendent upon the will of the governor,—the king's
creature; while to the sheriffs, creatures of the governor, was entrusted the selection of jurors.   Thus
almost all officers were to be made creatures of the
royal will.   Besides, England itself proposed to take
custody of the more important cases at law, trans-
porting alleged offenders for trial.   But the heaviest
blow at our liberties, which these acts proposed, was
the destruction of the town meeting, as a theatre for
the expression of opinion and public discussion.   It
was decreed that no meetings should be held, saving
for the election of municipal officers, except by express consent of the royal governor; and that only
such matters as he allowed should be discussed.

The people saw that their ancient liberties were
departing, and that time honored customs were being
. disallowed more and more; and they determined upon
resistance.   "We broke no chain;" said Mr. Dana in

his oration at the Lexington Centennial, "we prepared to strike down any hand that might attempt to
lay one upon us. There was not one institution, law,
or custom, political or social, from the mountain top
to the sea-shore, which we cared to change. We
were then content to go on as parts of the British
empire, holding that slack and easy allegiance we always held, on the old terms of self-government and
home rule." But that was not to be allowed, and
our people determined to resist encroachments. Already, even before these last acts subversive of the
chartered rights of the province, our honored townsman, Major Hawley, at that time a leading member
of the colonial assembly, had become convinced of the
necessity for action ; and had publicly declared that,
"if the people would maintain their rights and liberties, they must fight for them."

For the sake of concert of action and public utter-
ance, meetings of the people were everywhere held.
Those assembling put themselves in peril; for in so
doing they set the new law at defiance. Berkshire
held a Congress at Stockbridge, and took a noble and
patriotic stand in regard to the evils that threatened
our liberties. Among their recommendations was
one that the 14th of July should be observed as a day
of fasting and prayer, "to implore the Divine assist-
ance that He would interpose and in mercy avert those
evils with which we are threatened." A Pittsfield
town meeting declared that they viewed it of the
greatest importance to the well being of the province,
that the people of it "*utterly refuse the least submission
to the said acts, and, on no consideration to counte-
nance the taking place of those acts among us, but resist them to the last extremity.*"

To this period belongs an unsigned paper found among the documents of Col. Elisha Porter of Hadley, to which I have been kindly allowed access. "Voted, that we will never take, hold, exercise, or execute, any commission, office, or employment whatever, under, by virtue of, or in any manner derived from, any authority pretended, or attempted to be given, by a late act of the British Parliament, entitled 'An Act for the Better Regulating of the Government of the Province of Massachusetts Bay in New England;' and that we will heartily concur with the people of this county and province, in using our utmost endeavors to maintain, secure, and defend, the charter, and constitutional rights of the people of this province; and transmit them inviolate to posterity."

I hazard the opinion that this was a copy, or perhaps first draft, of a vote passed in a Hadley town meeting, which sent delegates to a convention of Hampshire County, held in Northampton, September 22 and 23, 1774, "to consult upon measures to be taken in this time of general distress in the province, occasioned by the late attacks of the British ministry upon the constitution of said province."

The president of this convention was Timothy Danielson of Brimfield, who had just had the honor, with thirteen others, among them John Adams and James Bowdoin, to be rejected from the council by Governor Gage, after an election by the General Court; and who, with others, is mentioned by Bradford, after the Otises, father and son, Samuel Adams, and Major Hawley, as among the leaders in opposing the arbitrary measures of the British ministry.

This convention passed, with great unanimity, a series of resolutions, in which they declared that the

county did not intend to withdraw from the king; but
that the charter of the province ought to be kept inviolate. The resolutions also characterized the acts
of the British Parliament as "subversive," and the
acts of Governor Gage, the rightfulness of whose authority they doubted, as destructive of their rights;
declared the holding of a Provincial Congress at Concord to be necessary, as well as the holding of town
meetings; and exhorted the people to be diligent to
acquaint themselves with the military art, under the
direction of such persons as they might choose, and
to furnish themselves with arms and ammunition.
Conventions, with similar results, were held in most
of the other counties in the State. Thus, while the
people of our county declared their wish to be loyal
to their sovereign, they also showed their determination to maintain their vested and ancestral rights,
even if, as Hawley had declared and as seemed likely,
a resort to arms must be taken. *

The necessity of a Provincial Congress, which the
Convention declared, arose, in part, from the fact that
the General Court had not been held for some time;
and that, if held, it was liable to be prorogued at any
time, by the governor. Delegates, having been appointed, assembled in Salem in October, 1774; chose
John Hancock president; and adjourned to Concord.

Our members of that Congress were Dea. Elias Lyman of Southampton, and Col. Seth Pomeroy of
Northampton, a veteran who had served under Pep-
perell at the reduction of Louisburg. The latter was
a member of the committee who were directed to pre-
pare an address to Governor Gage, and one of three
general officers who were chosen to command the
military of the province. Another of the three was

Colonel Ward, who afterwards held general command at the time of the Battle of Bunker Hill, and who was made one of the first four major-generals by the Continental Congress. The third was Colonel Thomas who held command at Roxbury on that memorable day. Colonel Thomas, Colonel Pomeroy, and Colonel Heath, also of our colony, were three of the first eight brigadier-generals of the Continental army.

This first Provincial Congress also appointed a committee of safety with executive powers. They also directed municipal tax officers not to pay money to the treasurer of the province, who was under the influence of the governor; but to Henry Gardner, Esq., whom they constituted receiver-general. Ours was the first town to respond, paying to Treasurer Gardner, by the hand of Major Hawley, the first money he had received. At this time, Belchertown "voted by a great majority, to defend the constables, both in collecting their taxes, (as some threaten in this day of calamity, now all law is stopped and all executive authority is put down,) and in paying over the money when collected, to said Gardner."

The standing committee appointed by the Provincial Congress, many of whom were military officers, were directed to ascertain the quantity of arms, cannon, and gunpowder in the province, and to encourage military discipline among the citizens. Militia companies were speedily organized everywhere, and the people determined to be ready for armed resistance. Southampton showed its determination to be ready, by voting a sum of money for some person to instruct the Minute Men in learning the military art; also to give the Minute Men ninepence a time, for six half days in learning military exercises.

To the point of armed resistance, events were rapidly tending. In February, 1775, Parliament declared Massachusetts in rebellion. The instructions of Dartmouth to Governor Gage were, "The sovereignty of the king over the colonies requires a full and absolute submission." To this Gage replied, "The time for conciliation is over; the forces must take the field;" and he called for twenty thousand soldiers, to enforce the "subversive" acts of Parliament. Meetings of the people were still held, some of which Gage attempted to disperse by his soldiers. Massachusetts was under martial law. The spirit of the people was resolute and undaunted. The issue was fairly made up. Neither party would retire; and on the 19th of April the collision came at Lexington and Concord; with what results the country knows; and all the world knows; for the first shot was heard around the world.

The Provincial Congress had adjourned to May; but its Committee of Safety, in pursuance of their executive powers, at once convened it; and it proceeded to adopt those measures which were "indispensable for the salvation of the country," one of which they deemed to be the raising of an army of thirty thousand men. They called for nearly half that number from this State. The committee had already, by circular, urged the towns to lose no time in sending troops to Boston. "Our all is at stake;" they said, "every minute is infinitely precious." The appeal met a prompt response. Men flew at once to arms. A few brief hours, after receipt of the tidings, sufficed to start a company from many a town. Hampshire was not behind her sister counties. Col. Timothy Danielson of Brimfield, whom Gage had recently rejected from sitting in the council, led a Hampshire regiment to meet Gage in arms.

In this regiment was the Northampton company of sixty-nine men, commanded by Capt. Jonathan Allen, and Lieuts. Oliver Lyman and James Shepherd. The Southampton company of forty-six men, a few of whom were from Northampton and Norwich, was commanded by Capt. Lemuel Pomeroy, and Lieut. Jonathan Wales. Nine days after the battle, Southampton voted " to do something to support our friends and brethren that have gone into the army." " Voted to pay for two-thirds of the provision that is provided for Capt. Lemuel Pomeroy's company." A committee of nine was chosen to collect the provision and dispatch it by team.

Capt. Abel Thayer of Williamsburg could not wait for his company, and hastened for the scene of action with ten men, where he was joined by twenty-one others. The other towns were equally zealous. Col. Ruggles Woodbridge of South Hadley, commanded a Hampshire regiment, part of which served with the gallant Prescott within the redoubt at Bunker Hill.

At midday, April 21, tidings reached Berkshire, and the next morning Colonel Patterson of Lenox was leading to Boston a regiment of northern Berkshire men, completely armed and equipped, and mostly uniformed. At Bunker Hill this regiment built and defended Fort No. 3 in Charlestown; aided in the siege of Boston till its surrender; proceeded thence to Canada via. New York; retreated with the army to Ticonderoga where it fortified Mount Independence; rejoined Washington in New Jersey; crossed the Delaware with him, and fought at Princeton and Trenton; and was in at Burgoyne's surrender; thus serving through the whole period most gallantly and with fearful losses.

Bunker Hill convinced both parties that there was mettle in the provincials. This was a revelation to the British, and an inspiration to the continental leaders and people. One of the events of that glorious day is matter of local pride to us. Colonèl Pomeroy, the veteran of eighty years, was early on the field, a volunteer like Warren, without a command. When the day was lost, he was among the last to leave the field; and, waving his shattered musket, he sought, as Putnam was also doing, (but both of them in vain,) to rally the troops upon Bunker Hill, after they had been driven, without ammunition, from the entrenchments on Breeds Hill.

In July, 1775, the Continental Congress declared: "Our cause is just, our union is perfect, our internal resources are great, and we solemnly declare, before God and the world, that, exerting all the means and power which our Creator hath bestowed, we will employ the arms, which our implacable enemies have compelled us to use, with unabating perseverance, and at every hazard, for the preservation, of our liberties, being resolved to die free men, rather than live slaves. But we have not raised an army with the ambitious design of separating from Great Britain and establishing independent States."

The logic of events is mightier than the purposes of men. Our people did not intend independence at that time. But God intended independence, and in his good time it came. "Whom the gods will destroy they first make mad." The king and his ministry were madly bent upon subjugating the colonies, and they would hear to nothing short of it. They employed troops of hireling soldiers from the continent. They sought to stir up the merciless savages of our forests to butcher and scalp us. By such measures they rapidly drove the people to resolve upon separation.

No one can fail to notice the correspondence between Independence and Emancipation, in this particular. Neither was at first intended by the people, who were God's instruments in effecting them; but the course of events, and a good Providence, drove us to both.

Gradually the minds of the leaders of public opinion in Massachusetts, had been drawing toward the conclusion that the true course was to strike for absolute independence. When they urged the idea upon their brethren in the States to the southward, they did not always meet a favorable response. But the king and his ministry were their best allies, constantly furnishing them with fresh arguments. The transfer of the theater of war to New York and the South, was most opportune in preparing the way for this event. The act of Parliament interdicting trade with all the colonies, and making their goods upon the high seas liable to seizure and forfeit, and their persons to impressment, conspired, with other acts, to hasten the decision.

All this while the clergy were lending their powerful aid to the patriotic cause. The Provincial Congress urged that they should adapt their discourses to the times. This they were not slow to do. Their sermons breathed the spirit of freedom, and not seldom were powerful philippics against their oppressors. Their prayers were powerful with God in procuring his intervention, for they were men of faith. "We have from our pulpits," says Thatcher, "most fervent and pious effusions to the throne of divine grace, in behalf of our bleeding, afflicted country." At one of their annual gatherings, they sent an address to the Provincial Congress, expressing their "sympathy for the distresses of their much injured and oppressed country," and commending them and the army to the protection and guidance of God. After a fearless election sermon by Gad Hitchcock of Pembroke, from the words "when the righteous are in authority the people rejoice, but when the wicked bear rule the people mourn," Gage refused the request of the assembly to order a fast, alleging that "the request was only to give an orportunity for sedition to flow from the pulpit." The clergy, in turn, refused to stultify themselves, when he requested them to render thanks to God that their liberties had been preserved to them. Edward Everett says of them, that they "rendered services second to no others, in enlightening and animating the popular mind on the great question at issue."

During the intense excitement in Boston over the Stamp Act, Rev. Jonathan Mahew, pastor of the West church, denounced the act with unmitigated severity. Of Rev. Dr. Cooper of Brattle Street, pastor of Hancock, Warren, and many other leaders of the people, the *London Political Register* for 1780, says: "though a minister of peace, and, to all outward appearance, a meek and heavenly man, yet he was one of the chief instruments in stirring up the people to take arms." The annual election sermons of this period, preached before the Governor and General Court, are specimens of patriotic address, which em-

phatically attest the courage, patriotism, and foreseeing wisdom of the authors.

Nor were they content with uttering their sentiments
only in the pulpit. They were always present in the
town meetings, aiding in the deliberations and decisions of the people. They encouraged the people as
they went forth to do battle in the just cause. Em-
erson of Concord, rallying and encouraging his parishioners in the gray dawn of that eventful morning
which made Lexington and Concord household words,
is a sample of our clergy of that day, not many of
whom had his opportunity, though many of them had
his spirit. They were ever ready as chaplains, or
even as soldiers, to encounter the perils of the field.

At this very time of which we are speaking, Rev.
Robert Breck, for almost half a century pastor of the
old First Church in Springfield, though sixty-two
years of age, was with Colonel Porter's Hampshire
regiment, amid the snows of Canada, with Arnold and
Wooster, seeking in vain to retrieve the disaster of
Montgomery's defeat and heroic death. Colonel
Porter's diary repeatedly mentions him; now preaching, though opportunities in that fearful campaign
were rare; now accompanying him to confer with
other officers; now leaving the regiment and going to
spend a few days with the sick at Fort George at the
head of Lake George. Long before the collision came
Rev. Jonathan Judd of Southampton, pastor of some of
our people, had shown his patriotism and readiness to
share the sacrifices of his parishioners, by sending to
them a communication in which he says, " if such a
day of difficulty and distress should come," (referring
to the operation of the Stamp Act,) " I will join with
a committee of yours; and they and I will reduce

the salary as low as it can be reasonably thought proper." When the " day of difficulty and distress" came, the pastor was, no doubt, ready for his share of sacrifice.

Several months before the declaration, Massachusetts refused to recognize the king's authority, in the caption of public documents; and these were accordingly issued in the name of the Government and the people. In May, 1776, the legislature passed an order calling on the people to express their opinion as to formal and entire separation from Great Britain; and requesting them to instruct their representatives.

The responses were not equivocal. The record of one of our towns shall serve as a sample. " At a full meeting of the inhabitants of Belchertown, held at the. meeting-house, June 25, 1776, Dea. Aaron Lyman was chosen moderator. The question was put by the moderator, whether, should the honorable Continental Congress, for the safety of the United Colonies in America, declare their independence of the kingdom of Great Britain, they, the said inhabitants, would solemnly engage, with their lives and fortunes, to support them in the measure; and it passed in the affirmative by a universal vote." As did Belchertown so did Hampshire; so did Massachusetts, with substantial unanimity. They expressed their opinion; they instructed their representatives; but they, of course, referred the decision to the Continental Congress.

Many leading men wrote to the delegates in Congress, to urge the measure. And here the foresight and patriotism of Hampshire's great civilian, Major Hawley, shone with peculiar lustre. " Hawley," says Bancroft, " was the first to discern through the darkness, the coming national government of the republic, even while it still lay far below the horizon; and he wrote from Watertown, where the General Court was held, to Samuel Adams: 'The eyes of all this Continent are fastened on your body, to see whether you act with firmness and intrepidity, with the spirit and dispatch which our situation calls for. It is time for your body to fix on periodical, annual elections; nay, to form into a Parliament of two houses.'"

Samuel Adams also received a message from James Warren. "The king's silly proclamation will put an end to petitioning. Movements worthy of your august body are expected. A declaration of independence and treaties with foreign powers." "This intelligence will make a plain path for you, though a dangerous one," wrote Abigail Adams to her husband, John Adams. "Let us separate. Let us renounce them."

In an autograph letter of June 18th from Elbridge Gerry, one of our representatives in Congress, to Colonel Elisha Porter of Hadley, then in command of a Hampshire regiment in Canada, Gerry tells Porter: "Things are going on well in the colonies, in respect to independency, confederation, etc.; and the question relative to the former is to be agitated in Congress the 1st of July."

The eventful day came. All the colonies were represented. The delegates of each colony, except New York, had received full power of action. The debate upon the proposition was not concluded until the next day; when the delegates from twelve colonies, the thirteenth afterwards acceding, unanimously voted that "these colonies are, and of right ought to be, free and independent States."

Jefferson's draft of the declaration of the reasons for the act, and of the principles upon which they proposed to proceed, was debated and amended on the third, and was given to the world on the fourth. And so, for now a hundred years, we have stood before the world, free and united States. Let us give God the glory. Vain would have been the help of man. Futile would have been the efforts of patriot statesmen and patriot soldiers, except that a just God stretched out his arm of might to defend a just cause; and that a wise God gave foresight to the men, who, at that and in subsequent periods, have shaped our Government.

MAJOR JOSEPH HAWLEY.

The civil history of the period requires, as its complement, the military history, even as the statesmen could by no means have given us independence, if the people had refused to fight. But before I sketch our part in these gloomy events, I would pay an additional word of passing tribute to Hampshire's great commoner, our townsman, Maj. Joseph Hawley. He was, probably, the foremost lawyer of the Hampshire bar at this time, though Colonel Worthington of Springfield, and Esquire Lyman of Suffield, (which was then in Hampshire,) were forensic foemen worthy of his steel. Through all this period he was a member of the General Court, and, as Hildreth says, the most influential of all the country members. Few had more to do than he in shaping the policy of the colony; in disputing with the royal governors their encroachments upon our rights; or in bringing to pass the final issue. Upon the repeal of the Stamp Act, Parliament *recommended*, and Governor Bernard *demanded* indemnity for the persons who had suffered in the riots consequent upon the attempted execution of the act. The matter was long pending, and frequently in hot dispute, in which the governor found Major Hawley one of his staunchest opponents. The firm resolves in answer to the governor's ungracious speech, and the bill which finally settled the matter, were prepared by James Otis, Jr., Samuel Adams, Samuel Dexter, and Joseph Hawley, of whom Bradford remarks: "They were the most active and influential patriots of that period."

In May, 1770, Hutchinson, acting governor, illegally ordered the General Court to meet in Cambridge instead of Boston. This provoked strong opposition, which was conducted especially by Samuel and John Adams, Major Hawley, and John Hancock.

In June, 1772, it was proposed that the governor and the superior judges should be paid from the treasury of Great Britain. The effect of this measure would have been to make all these officers indifferent to the voice of the representatives of the people. Of course it evoked hot opposition. The several messages to the governor from the house, upon this subject, were prepared by Major Hawley, Samuel Adams, John Hancock, W. Heath, and J. Warren.

In January, 1773, in a long address to the General Court, Hutchinson advocated the absolute supremacy of Parliament, whose mandates, he claimed, the colonies "ought to obey without hesitation or inquiry." Here again, in making up the reply of the house, the ability and resolution of Hawley were required. With him, in the preparation of the reply, were associated Samuel Adams, John Hancock, J. Foster, and William Philips. With Samuel Adams he had most friendly relations, to whom his legal knowledge and sound sense were often of great service.

When the Massachusetts delegates to the first Continental Congress were on their way to Philadelphia, at Springfield they received from the Hampshire statesman a note, in which he said: "We must fight, if we can not otherwise rid ourselves of British taxation. Fight we must finally, unless Britain retreats. Our salvation depends upon a persevering union. Every grievance of any one colony must be held as a grievance of the whole."

Nor was it only in opposition to England that his services were called into requisition. As an example of other services, it may be mentioned that a standing dispute of this period, between New York and ourselves, as to our boundary, was at length adjusted while he was chairman of the commission on the part of our State.

Bradford, in a brief description of the leaders of this period in our house of representatives, James Otis, Jr., Samuel Adams, Thomas Cushing, James Bowdoin, Samuel Dexter, Joseph Hawley, Thomas Saunders, and Joseph Gerrish, compares Hawley to Otis. "Ardent, zealous, and eloquent; and, in his writings against the friends of arbitrary power, full of severity and sarcasm." Of him, Dr. Dwight says : "He was one of the ablest and most influential men in Massachusetts Bay, for a considerable period before the Revolution—an event in which few men had more efficiency. He was a very able advocate. Many men have spoken with more eloquence and grace. I have never heard one speak with more force. His mind, like his eloquence, was grave, austere and powerful." The following good story is told of him

5

and his colleague in the General Court, Mr. Strong. (Probably Caleb Strong, then a young man just rising of thirty years of age, who had recently been admitted to the bar, but who afterwards became no less eminent than Hawley; serving twenty-five years as county attorney; several times in the Governor's council and State senate; member of the convention which framed the constitution; one of our first United States senators, to which position he was re-elected; and governor of the State eleven years, including the period of the second war with England, to which he, in common with the dominant party in the State, was opposed.)   Hawley, it seems, was subject to seasons of despondency.   On their return from the General Court at one time, he was deploring the poor prospect of success in the Revolutionary struggle.   " We shall both be hung," said he to Mr. Strong.   " No, Major Hawley," was the reply, " probably not more than forty will be hung; we shall escape."   " I'll have you to know," said Hawley, " that I am one of the first three," and the next day he made an eloquent and patriotic speech to his 'fellow-citizens.   And he was not so far wrong as many men are in their estimate of themselves.

At this time we were a part of Northampton, and have no local Revolutionary history, except what we have in common with that town and Southampton. The history of this patriot and statesman is, therefore, matter for just pride to us as a town; for he was our representative, sent to the General Court by the votes of our ancestors, whom he served in that body repeatedly, preferring to remain there rather than to sit in the council, to which he was several times elected by his colleagues.   Not that

Northampton can monopolize his fame. His name adds luster to old Hampshire and the whole Commonwealth; for he was one of the Revolutionary worthies.

1149143 ·

MILITARY HISTORY OF THE PERIOD.

But the story of our people's share in the military history must needs be told; for, though sad, it was patriotic, and was the inevitable sequel of the decisions of our civic leaders. The people were the ones who saw and felt the fighting. All honor to them, for their patient and heroic sacrifices.

Between the battles of Lexington and Bunker Hill, Ticonderoga had been captured. It seemed to Hawley and others, that the government ought to organize a force to hold the defensible positions about the lower Champlain, if nothing more; and they accordingly urged the measure. It was, on the whole, judged expedient to push northward rather than remain at lower Champlain; and thus to secure Canada if possible. Montgomery, one of the ablest of our generals, was placed in charge; and met victory till he reached Quebec. Here everything was against him. To co-operate with him, Washington had detached a portion of his own force about Boston, and sent them, under Arnold, by way of the Kennebec, and through the forests of Maine. Lemuel Bates and others from Southampton belonged to this expedition. One of Arnold's captains was a Hampshire man, Elihu Lyman, brother of Captain Josiah Lyman of Belchertown, of whom mention will soon be made. The march of Arnold was attended with incredible hardships, in the form of hunger, fatigue and cold, almost beyond endurance. Among the troops were some sailors, who became so ungovernable, that Captain, afterwards Major, Lyman was deputed to take them back to Boston. This he finally succeeded in doing, although many times on the homeward march his life was in great peril from them. Arnold at length reached Quebec, but with ranks greatly thinned, and with only five rounds of ammunition to a man. Montgomery soon joined him, but the combined force numbered not more than 1,200 men; and the time of many of these was soon to expire. To make the situation more deplorable, it was the dead of Winter. A desperate, and, as it proved, disastrous assault was made in the teeth of a howling storm, on the last night but one of 1775. The gallant Montgomery fell; and with him many brave men suffered death or capture. But the dauntless spirit of Arnold was not yet quelled; and he determined to maintain the siege as far as possible. Montgomery's fall roused the spirit of the colonists, who determined to retrieve the disaster.

Without waiting to consult Congress, Washington recommended Massachusetts, New Hampshire, and Connecticut, each to raise and send forward a regiment. The command of our regiment he gave to Col. Elisha Porter of Hadley, in a letter which Porter's descendants preserve as the most precious among numerous documentary relics of their ancestor. Washington desires him " to use the utmost diligence and dispatch possible, to complete the regiment, and march it into Canada by the shortest and best way, that, from your knowledge of the country, and from the best information you can get, you think will be the most expeditious. The necessity of reinforcing our troops posted, and forming the blockade of Quebec, is too apparent to need dwelling on. I would have you order each company to march as fast as they are raised, the whole putting themselves under command of the general or commanding officer in Canada, as fast as they arrive there."

This regiment was composed largely of Hampshire troops. The diary of Colonel Porter, covering a portion of their period of service, is a most interesting relic, among his papers. From it the following fragmentary extracts are made, since it gives an authentic picture of the times, which will be of interest to us; especially as some of our town's people form a part of the picture.

Porter's appointment was made January 19, 1776. For two months he was filling up the regiment, and dispatching companies to the front. February 4th, he went to Northampton, and gave orders to Captain Chapin and Lieutenant Hunt, who, it will be observed, commanded our company in the expedition. He got them off in advance of himself. March 22d, he got off Captain Josiah Lyman's, the Belchertown company. He himself set out the next day. About the 29th, he met a man, three weeks from Quebec, who had seen Captain Chapin's company at St. Johns. Made the passage from Skeenesborough (now Whitehall) to Ticonderoga in boats, he and Captains Lyman and Shepherd, with some of their men, cutting several miles through ice six inches thick. April 17th, set out from Ticonderoga with one hundred and forty-four men. Reached St. Johns on the 19th. Ordered by Arnold to join Wooster at Quebec, which they reached on the 27th, camping on the Plains of Abraham. Saw several of Captain Chapin's company,

which was five miles distant. All have had the small-
pox but William Clark; mostly recovered. Drew
ammunition. Carried ladders near to the walls, under cover of the fog. Under arms upon the heights.
General Thomas took command. Enemy about to
be strongly reinforced. Sent to Captain Chapin to
bring off his men at once. In line of battle on the
heights. Ordered to retreat. Marched fifteen miles.
Halted at 8 P. M. Intermittent sleep. Off at midnight. At sunrise got two loaves of bread for seventy men. Fired upon by ships. Marched thirty
miles. Men from hospital, scarce able to walk, with
the rest. Heavy cannonade. Can't make a stand
for want of provisions, and of everything but cannon. Sick men from Quebec return, except William
Clark of Captain Chapin's company, who was left dy-
ing. John Davis and Walker of the same company,
who were not able to be moved, doubtless perished.
Half allowance of meat to-day. No meat for three
days. Regiment ordered to St. Johns. Appointed
commander of the garrison at Chambly. General
Thomas dies of small-pox. Captain Chapin one of
the bearers. Heavy firing below St. Johns. General Thompson and others prisoners. Worked till
midnight with all my men, in getting up bateaux.
Rained very hard. Then turned in. By light turned
out on fatigue duty. Alarm in the afternoon.
Worked all night in hauling bateaux up the rapids.
Burnt the fort at Chambly. Marched to St. Johns.
Colonel Stark's and my regiment brought up the
rear. Council of War decides to retire to Crown
Point. One hundred and twenty-six of my regiment
sick. Had a present of fresh beef—a great rarity.
Not enough bateaux. Marched along the shore,

bringing up the rear. Lodged on the ground without a covering. Men in an ugly swamp. A good sermon by Mr. Breck. Clothing divided among the soldiers. July 16th received the agreeable news of independency being declared by the Congress. About noon, two or three kettles of brandy grog evidenced our joy at the news, which we expressed in proper toasts.

At this time they were at Crown Point, and reached Ticonderoga the next day, where the army was divided into four brigades, Porter's regiment being assigned to Arnold's brigade. Here Colonel Porter was frequently employed in courts-martial, in one of which Arnold was tried for some misdemeanor and reported to Congress. A little later, Capt. Joseph Lyman of Northampton arrived with a company of ninety-nine recruits. The diary ends August 25th, at which time Colonel Porter reports that many of his men were sick of fever and ague and other diseases.

When the men of this regiment returned I am not able to ascertain. But it is certain that Colonel Porter had a command at the surrender of Burgoyne a year later; and it is to be presumed that the regiment was recruited, and continued through the campaign, which culminated in the victory at Saratoga.

The Committees of Correspondence and Safety played an important part throughout the province, in the home management of affairs. They were appointed in every town, early in the great struggle, even before appeal was made to arms.

They looked after deserters and tories; they consulted for the public weal; and were in communication with both the civil and the military authorities, and with one another. As a specimen of the spirit with which they were appointed, the following vote, passed by Belchertown, may be given. Having appointed a committee of safety, February 9, 1775, "to confer with similar committees from other towns," it was "voted by a great majority, that, if we hear of any routs, riots, or other unlawful assemblies, we will immediately inform one or more of the committee, and will, in compliance to their advice, do anything that is reasonable, or within our power, to suppress them." It was also recommended, that, if they could not be otherwise suppressed, the aid of the committees from other towns be invoked. This favor they promised to reciprocate in case of need.

Northampton's first Committee of Correspondence, Inspection, and Safety, consisted of the following representative men : Maj. Joseph Hawley, Robert Breck, Ezra Clark, Dea. Josiah Clark, Jacob Parsons, Col. Seth Pomeroy, Elijah Hunt, Ephraim Wright, Elias Lyman, Lieut. Elijah Clark, Capt. Joseph Lyman, who afterwards led a company of recruits to join the northern army, Quartus Pomeroy, Martin Phelps, Caleb Strong, Jr., and Dr. Levi Shepherd.

There had, however, been a previous Committee of Correspondence, and also one of Inspection. These two were superseded by the new committee, which was to have the whole matter in hand.

The next committee consisted of the same persons, excepting that Abner Barnard and John Lyman were substituted for Col. Seth Pomeroy and Elijah Hunt.

The Southampton Committee of Safety consisted of Jonathan Judd, Jr., Samuel Burt, Elias Lyman, Aaron Clark, Jonathan Clark, Timothy Clark, Samuel Pomeroy, Samuel Clapp, and Israel Sheldon.

May 8, 1775, the Provincial Congress authorized the Committees of Correspondence and Selectmen of the towns, " to take effectual care to disarm all who will not give assurance of their good intentions in regard to the interests of the country," and to " put it out of their power to obstruct, by any means whatever, the necessary measures for the common defence." This was a precaution made necessary by the tory spirit, which here and there exhibited itself.

Local conventions of the Committees of Safety were occasionally held for mutual conference. One was held at Northampton, February 5, 1777, at which most of the towns of old Hampshire were represented. Nathaniel Dwight, chairman of Belchertown's committee, presided over the convention. They took into consideration the suffering condition of the northern army, and sought to stir up the Committee of Supplies to send relief. Various other recommendations were made, one of which was a petition to the General Court, to devise measures to suppress toryism. They complain of " our inimical brethren," who, it appears, sneered at the General Court; defied the selectmen to draft them; counterfeited the paper currency; paid no regard to the Committees of Safety; and endeavored to prevent the raising of a new levy of men.

A complaint made by Capt. Josiah Lyman of the Belchertown company in Colonel Porter's regiment, just before he set out for Canada, will illustrate this state of things. The document was addressed to the home Committee of Safety, of which Nathaniel Dwight, president of the aforesaid convention, was chairman, and, with sundry omissions, is as follows: " Josiah Lyman complains, and says that he was at

6

Ware, with orders from Colonel Porter to enlist men to join the regiment in the proposed expedition to Canada; and he and Luke Chapin having got seven men willing to enlist, Colonel —— tells them, that the head men of the town was no ways obliged to encourage their men to go, and appeared to talk discouraging about their enlisting. Colonel ——'s son Moses said Colonel Porter was a d—d Tory, and he had as lief go under Tom Gage as go under him, and that he would not go under him if he might be his lieutenant-colonel. Colonel —— said he had some scruples upon his mind about him. I, the said Josiah, queried why he voted for Porter to go to Canada. He said he did not think he was a Tory, but that he was too fierce and heady. In all which I, the said Josiah, think I was much injured and abused."

Luke Chapin, and several other eye-witnesses of the affair, confirm Captain Lyman's charges. Whether anything was ever done about it is not known. At this time, the aforesaid Colonel —— was in command of the Fourth Hampshire regiment of militia, but was superseded by Colonel Porter upon his return from active service. That his arraignment of Porter was unjust, the confidence of Washington in Porter, as well as his own supersedure, abundantly proves. His motive was, probably, not Toryism, but personal jealousy; for he seems to have retained the confidence of his townsmen, so far that he was afterwards influential in town affairs.

All accounts agree that the northern army suffered severe hardships. They were insufficiently supplied with clothing, and were often short of food. Small-pox and fevers ravaged the army fearfully. Of the garrison at Ticonderoga, a few months after the period covered by Porter's diary, Bancroft says: "The sick were very numerous and perishing in misery, and all suffered from want of clothing." There was, also, some lack of discipline, and consequently of efficiency, owing partly to the short terms of enlistment, and partly to the independent spirit of the citizen soldiers, who were patriotic, but had not fully learned the need of subordination in military affairs.

On account of the hardship to be endured, desertions were frequent; and here the services of the Committees of Safety were called into requisition by the officers in the field. There is preserved among Colonel Porter's papers, a letter to himself from Major Hawley, chairman of our Committee of Safety. It is interesting, as showing the current state of affairs, the functions of the Committees of Safety, the motive and spirit of the deserters, and the attitude of the people towards them. It is dated July 7, 1776, and is as follows: "Sir:—Mr. Breck lately received a letter from Captain Chapin and Lieutenant Hunt," (who were in command of our men in Porter's regiment,) "informing him that several of their company had deserted. We immediately wrote to the committees of every place where we thought they might secrete themselves, requesting the most effectual measures to secure them; but before they could have heard of it, those of this town came home. When called before the committee, they declared their design to return back, as soon as they could properly furnish themselves with the necessary apparel; and mentioned the want of it as the occasion of their deserting. They desired the committee to fix the time of their return. From a consideration of their circumstances, we permitted them to stay till this day.

"We heard that those from Southampton were to be at Worthington at a particular time, and sent to apprehend them; but are now convinced that they had no design to secrete themselves. They readily engaged to return, and said they always intended to; and seemed extremely sorry for their indiscretion. As they have all conducted well heretofore, and are persons of good reputation, we wish and request on their behalf, that the greatest lenity may be shown them. The disapprobation of their conduct among their friends has been some degree of punishment; and we beg leave to say that we imagine a temporary shame for misconduct, in minds that are ingenuous, will sometimes produce better effects than punishment attended with lasting infamy."

We, certainly, have no occasion to judge them more severely than did Major Hawley. Many things may be excused in a half-clad, poorly-fed soldier. The case was a desperate one, and no wonder that faith sometimes failed.

Colonel Porter's regiment set out for Canada in the midst of the early snows of 1776. On the 25th of June, in the same year, the General Court ordered five thousand troops to be raised for six months' service. The Hampshire troops were to reinforce the northern army, and were offered each a bounty of £7. The quota of old Hampshire was seven hundred and fifty-four; of these, Northampton was to send forty-seven, and Southampton seventeen. Shortly after, other regiments were ordered from Hampshire and Berkshire, to join the northern army. In September, Washington called for more of the militia;

and the General Court ordered every fifth man to march. Nor was this enough. In December, one-eighth of the Hampshire militia were ordered to join Schuyler and Gates. Bradford, in his History of Massachusetts, remarks: "Nothing but a devoted spirit of patriotism, and a strong love of liberty, could have prompted to such sacrifices and efforts. In other times, the expenses and exertions of the year 1776 alone, would have discouraged the inhabitants. The greater part of the whole male population was engaged in the public service in the course of the year. It also required large numbers to attend the wagons of provisions and stores, and ship carpenters were sent to the lake to build boats; and women and children were obliged to perform the ordinary labor of agriculture."

These were stirring times; and it is to be regretted that we have so incomplete a record of the names of the soldiers who served the country during this period; though it seems that it must have included nearly the whole able-bodied male population.

As an instance of this, it may be related that Jonathan Clapp, son of Major Jonathan and brother of Quartermaster Benjamin, who ran the grist mill on the Manhan, had been compelled to resist his impulses to join the army, in order to serve the people at home as a miller, there being no other in the region. But as news came, in 1777, that the conflict was approaching between our army and Burgoyne, he could no longer resist his impulses; and so he locked his mill and hastened towards the seat of conflict, though he was too late for the engagement.

At the time of the battle of Bennington, which

had shortly preceded Burgoyne's defeat, his father, Major Jonathan, who was in some public service, lay sick in Pittsfield, in care of the other son, Benjamin. The roar of the artillery was distinctly heard in Pittsfield, and filled the son with such ardor, that nothing but the extreme necessity of his father prevented him from rushing off for the fray.

Who led those companies from the Hamptons, which followed Captain Chapin's company of Porter's regiment, during the northern campaign, I am unable to say, saving that the Northampton records, in 1777, speak of " the men who went with Capt. Joseph Lyman to Ticonderoga last Summer." It will be remembered that Porter, in his diary, speaks of the arrival of these men. It appears, also, that one, Captain Allen, led another company; for, early in 1777, the town voted that " the persons who shall now engage in the service aforesaid, who belonged to Captain Allen's company and Captain Chapin's company the last year, both officers and privates, shall have full compensation for all losses by them sustained in clothes and other articles." Each of these, and any others who would enlist, were to be paid a bounty of £15.

It was at this time reported, that some citizens had failed to do their proper share in promoting the public cause; and accordingly the town chose a committee to see who were delinquent, and to assess them such sums as they judged to be their share. The clerks of the militia companies were to collect this money. Northampton appears at that time to have had four militia companies; and the committee on delinquents in the fourth, which must have been our company, were Capt. David Lyman, Jonathan Janes, Samuel

Judd, David Chapman, and Joel Parsons. These, it will be noticed, are Easthampton names.

At this time, it was seen to be of great importance, that the enlistments be for three years, in order that the armies might not be liable to be crippled in a crisis, by the expiration of the soldiers' terms. Enlistments for this term proceeded very slowly; and the full levy was not secured till orders were issued for the several towns to raise their proportion by classes, making each class responsible for a man. The recruiting authorities were to make as good terms as they could with the men. The records of Northampton show that this course was taken here. How many, or who, Easthampton sent is not known; but she must have sent her quota.

It was voted at that time, to allow each man, who had or who would enlist for three years, or during the war, £30; and to pay to certain marines a bounty of £10 for two years, and of £10 more for another year. If the families of soldiers in the Continental army were in need, it was voted to see them supplied.

April 23, 1777, two battalions of seven hundred and fifty men each, were ordered from Hampshire County, for two months' service around Ticonderoga. This would have required nearly one hundred men from Northampton. But the cup was not even yet full. The formidable advance of Burgoyne in August, demanded larger sacrifices. Berkshire and Hampshire, and afterward other counties, were ordered to send on reinforcements. This levy called out every seventh man in the militia. Large sums were expended in provisioning the troops, and in making passable the roads over our western hills.

Great must have been the rejoicing of our people, when, at length, tidings came of the severe but victorious battles about Saratoga, and of the capitulation of Burgoyne on the 19th of October. I can never, however, think of the rejoicings of the victors, without thinking, too, of the heartache of those, by the blood of whose friends the victory was won. Who of our townsmen fell at Saratoga, I can not tell. But I make no doubt, that some hearts among us ached, when the brave victors returned ; but for all that it was matter for great rejoicing. The great nightmare, which had rested upon the breast of the State for more than a twelvemonth, was shaken off. The pet scheme of our enemies had failed. The immense drain upon the resources of the State would now, in some measure, be checked. The militia, some of whom had been long from home, were returned to their homes. Their immediate object was accomplished ; but the war was by no means over.

Burgoyne and his soldiers were conducted to Boston, whence, on parole, they sailed to England. Their route to the sea-board lay through Northampton and Hadley. Burgoyne was in custody of Colonel Porter, at whose house he spent a night. It is a fact of interest that that house is still occupied by Colonel Porter's descendants.

The war wore on, with its varied success and defeat ; with its heavy drafts of men and military supplies. But the towns nobly responded to the calls. In the year 1778, there were several calls. On the 20th of April, requisition was made upon Massachusetts for two thousand men, to recruit her fifteen decimated battalions in the Continental army. Hampshire's share was two hundred and forty-two ; Northampton's thirteen. On the same day, one thousand five hundred were ordered for the North River and Rhode Island, of which Hampshire was to furnish one hundred and eighty-two. Later in the year, this county had to furnish, for service in Rhode Island, and with General Stark at Albany, one hundred each. These calls would have required about thirty-three men from Northampton during the year.

The year 1779 saw no lightening of the burden. On the 8th of June, the county was asked for one hundred and two men for seven months' service in Rhode Island; and for two hundred and twenty-eight nine months' men to recruit again her fifteen battalions. On the 9th of October, she was asked for four hundred and fifty, to co-operate with the forces sent by our ally, France. To each of these men was given, besides their regular Continental pay, a bounty of £16 per month; and to the latter, a bonus of £30 also, and 2s. mileage. It must be remembered that, by this time, paper was at a discount. The records show that Northampton bravely did her share of the work of this year. Repeated assemblies were held to institute measures for meeting the call. Now the town was borrowing money to pay the bounty; now instructing the selectmen to get the men on as good terms as possible, but to get them at all events; here a reference to those who went to Providence, and to those who went with Captain Cook to New London; and there an order that a certain part of the bounty be paid in wheat at 4s., or "rie" at 3s., or corn at 2s. a bushel.

Although we know the burden of a four years' war, we are not fully able to realize the burden of an eight years' war, a part of it almost within hearing.

As the burden became heavier, men would stay at home if drafted, and pay a fine instead.

And it was not only men, but money, clothing and food, which were needed. At that time we had no factories. Our mothers carded and spun the wool, dyed the yarn, knit it into stockings, or wove it into blankets for the bed, or into cloth from which they cut and made the garments. When anything of this kind was needed, requisition was laid upon the towns. Committees were frequently appointed, either to solicit or in some cases with power to make such demands as they judged proportionate, upon the various families. Many times, blankets were cheerfully taken from beds in use. In 1778–9 and 80, orders were passed for the collection of shirts, shoes, and stockings; in one instance equal in number to one-seventh the males; in another to one-tenth the number of males over sixteen, and half as many blankets. In one case Northampton's share of each was sixty-four; and in another about forty, and half as many blankets. And Southampton's share was about half as many. In the call of 1780, Elijah Hunt of Northampton, was agent for Hampshire County. In 1778, a committee was appointed to go from house to house through the town, to collect "such things as they judged would be serviceable to the soldiers." These were to be sent to Albany "for the soldiers who went from this town." Jonathan Janes was the solicitor in our section of the old town. August 9, 1779, £1,500 were voted to pay for clothing for the Continental army, and on November 9, £1,678. At the same time they appointed a committee to purchase grain for the army. In 1780, a supply of beef was ordered, and Northampton voted to purchase, upon its credit, eleven thousand three hundred and sixty pounds. As showing the depreciation of the currency at this time, it may be mentioned that Belchertown's quota of beef was six thousand three hundred and sixty pounds, for which they had to pay £7,362. The records of Belchertown show three several calls for beef within a year.

One of the interesting and somewhat odd things on record as to those times, is the fact of the appointment of the following distinguished citizens as a committee " to procure cotton and linen rags, for the necessary purpose of making paper:" Simeon Parsons, Levi Shepherd, Benjamin Tappan, John Lyman, Maj. Jonathan Clapp.

Inasmuch as it had been noticed, " that many persons have hoarded up great stores, for which they asked exorbitant prices, which tends to discourage the soldiers, wrong the poor, and ' sinque' the continental currency," the four New England States, by a conference of committees, sought to fix the price of the necessaries of life. Their recommendations, ratified by the several legislatures, fixed the prices in the market centers. Massachusetts allowed local modification of the same.

This was in 1777 ; and in 1779, another State Convention was held in Concord, to regulate prices ; also a local convention in Northampton, " to agree upon a uniformity in the price of the articles, in the several towns in the County." Upon the basis of the agreement of 1777, Belchertown agreed upon a list of prices, which was probably essentially like that of the sister towns in this valley. It will be interesting to note a few of the most important or unique items.

Prices of labor. Farm hands, in haying or harvest,

not to exceed 3s. a day, and their dinner. A man, and two yoke of oxen, in the Spring, 6s. a day. Carpenters, 3s. 8d. a day. Women tailors, 1s. a day. Housemaids, 3s. a week. Man's board, 6s. a week. " A dinner at the tavern, without cyder to drink with it, 10d." Farm produce. Rye, 4s., corn, 3s., peas and beans, 6s., potatoes, 1 to 1⅓s. a bushel. Fresh pork, 4d., beef, 3½d., mutton and veal, 2½d., cheese, 6d., butter, 8d , wool, 2s. per pound. Yard wide flannel, cotton, and linen, 3s. 6d. a yard. Best men's shoes, 8s. a pair. This was a legislative, anti-monopoly movement. What effect it had, the town records at least, do not state.

We regret that we have not a more complete record of the names of the soldiers of the Revolutionary period. But men were too busy then with doing, to think very much about recording their deeds.

We of this town should be especially glad if we knew who, in the district which afterwards was made Easthampton, to remember as our representatives in the great struggle ; though we do not ascribe to the soldiers all the glory. The whole people shared in the hardships of the period. Especially was this true of the period which culminated with the surrender of Burgoyne. Everything not absolutely essential to the support of those at home, was then sent to the army. But though all the people shared the hardships, we should be glad to know who rendered actual military service; but our desire can be only in part gratified.

I have been able to find no record of the names of Northampton's soldiers, and we are left only to the statements handed down from that time by word of mouth. Putting these together, Rev. Luther Wright, in a note appended to his Historical Sketch of East-hampton, says: "Among those engaged more or less in the service of their country, were Captain Joseph Clapp and Quartermaster Benjamin Clapp, Dr. Stephen Wood, and his sons Daniel and David; the father died in the service at West Point. John Clapp, who was in the army four years, Benjamin Lyman, Jr., Stephen Wright, Jr., David Clapp, who never returned, Levi Clapp, Eliakim Clark, afterwards captain, Barzilar Brewer, and Willet Chapman. The last two died in the army. Moses Gouch served through the war."

I can add only the names of Phinehas Clark, Zadoc Danks, Stephen Wright, the father of Samuel Brooks, formerly of this town, and Daniel Braman.

On a previous page, I have spoken of the service of Major Jonathan Clapp and his sons, Jonathan and Benjamin. The latter was out twice, once with Washington at and about White Plains, N. Y. Two of Burgoyne's captured soldiers were, for a time, quartered with him in Easthampton. They were men of education and good parts. On one occasion, during his absence, his wife asked one of them to say grace at the table. This he did, and, somewhat irreverently, characterized the dish of meat as "bones," and his host as a rebel. Such trifling did not suit the Puritan and patriotic wife; and, on the return of her husband, they were treated to a good round lecture, and given to understand that it did not become prisoners to be too captious.

Phinehas Clark was, on one occasion, stationed as a guard on an important post, when an officer undertook to persuade him to allow him to pass without the countersign, urging that his business was most important. But the guard halted him by the deter-

mined threat to pierce him with his bayonet in case
of further advance; whereat the officer, who was
Washington in disguise, revealed himself, and expressed himself as satisfied with the guard's soldierly
conduct.   On another occasion, when he was ill, he
was placed on guard; and was overcome by sleep.
He was arrested and tried by court-martial; but his
illness (which should have exempted him from duty)
and his youth, were plead in extenuation so warmly,
by his comrades of Northampton, that his life was
spared; and he received only the nominal punishment of a day in the guard-house.   It is said that the
confinement probably saved his life, as the day was
so excessively hot that many on duty were fatally
sun-struck.

Benjamin Lyman, Jr., was the first of our citizens
to enlist in the Continental army, which he did at the
age of sixteen years.   He was in the battle of Bennington.   The story is preserved among his descendants that he was acting as a scout at the time of
the capture of Major Andre; and that he helped to
conduct Andre to head-quarters, holding the rope in
his hands while Andre was pinioned.   During the
night, while they were traveling, Andre stumbled
over some obstacle and fell, after which he complained
of having suffered injury by the fall.   On this account
young Lyman gave him a little looser rope.   He was
also one of those who kept guard at the sad time of
Andre's execution.

It is said that while in the army, he became so accustomed to the use of tainted meat, that, in after
years, he frequently allowed meat to become tainted
before eating it, though he could never get any to
quite equal that after which he was patterning.

These figures and facts, which I have been seeking to set before you, meant more to our fathers than they do to you. The statistics I have given, may be dull as you hear them to-day; but they interested them profoundly. If one hundred men were wanted to-day from Easthampton, some of you would be compelled to clothe yourself in blue, and take the musket in your hand. Some of you would soon be saying a last farewell to these smiling fields, to these grand old hills, to these pleasant homes, and to those in them whom you dearly love. You know, some of you, what these farewells mean; though, by a good Providence, they were not to you last farewells. But a four years' war does not drag so heavily as does an eight years' war; and though we suffered in the war for the Union, our sufferings and sacrifices were eclipsed by those of our fathers, in the war for Independence. And we ought to remember them gratefully, and cherish the record of their deeds.

The men of that day were men of profound trust in God. Joseph Hawley, for instance, was a man of earnest piety as well as of ardent patriotism. When the faint-hearted suggested in 1774, "Don't put off the boat till you know where you will land," Hawley's confident reply was, "God will bring us to a safe harbor." "Their energy," says a historian of the period, "was derived from their sense of the divine power."

This looking to God as their Sovereign, made our fathers dare to break with England at the outset; and brought them to this country. This controlled the spirit of their sons of the Revolutionary period, and made them set *right* above title and authority. They went to the peculiar and trying duties of those years

of strife and sacrifice, with seriousness and acknowledgment of God, as though they were to engage in
acts of worship. Their confidence in God sustained
their courage. It was God who gave them wisdom to
frame the form of government which they gave to
posterity. It was through the unseen pilotage of
God, that the ship of State sailed safe through the
perils of the early days of the Republic. Let us
never forget that God is the source of national security. He it is who must pilot us, as He piloted our
fathers, or we shall go to wreck. The proneness of
man to forget God, or ignore his personal agency, is
one of our great dangers. As a nation, we have had
marvelous material prosperity. Never, since the world
stood, has so large a territory been subjugated and
peopled, in so short a time. The fertility of inven-
tion has operated to make the fertility of the soil
available. The methods of tillage and of manufacture have been revolutionized in a way greatly to
enhance the power of any individual over nature,
and enabling each one to harness to his own uses
far more of nature's forces than in the days of our
fathers. The power of swift locomotion and of in-
stantaneous communication, gives us the world for a
market, and enables us to feel the pulse of all na-
tions. The influx of population from foreign lands
has largely increased the material resources of the
nation, though at some risk. Our institutions have
stood great and repeated strains. We stand strong
to-day, notwithstanding that multitudes have departed
from God. We have strength, and seem likely to en-
dure far into the future. We are at peace with the
world, whom we have invited to meet us in a friendly
contest in the industrial, and some of the fine arts, in

the city where our fathers, one hundred years ago
to-day, published to mankind their Declaration of
Independence.

Now, in contemplating this wonderful growth, and
this amazing expansion of our power, there is danger
that our thoughts will rest too exclusively upon material greatness; that we shall exalt skill in workman-
ship, and wealth of resources too highly. We may,
perhaps, feel undue security as to the perpetuity of
the Republic, because it has endured the searching
tests of one hundred years. But we have not yet so
far stood the test of time, that our institutions are
placed beyond contingency. One hundred and seventy-five years before the fatal night of Chaldea,
Isaiah prophesied her impending fate. But she con-
tinned, in reckless disregard of the warning, to court
her doom. All this while, at least until near the last,
she was steadily increasing in material greatness.
But in one night Babylon fell; and from that time
forth the Chaldean became a vassal.

Let us not be over secure. If the Republic is to
continue its beneficent existence, it will be because of
the virtue and piety of the people.

Nothing is more demonstrable from history, than
that a predominantly material civilization speedily
becomes a corrupt civilization. And such a civilization is neither the nurse nor conservator of republics;
but is the mother of abominations, and the foe of the
best interests of men. Therefore, it is most important, that the young men and women, who are to-day
in training to become pillars in society, should be
taught that a nation's highest interests are not material, but immaterial; that virtue is of more consequence than fortune; that intellectual attainment is a

8

worthier object of endeavor than physical gratifica-
tion ; that manhood is better than money ; that it is
better to lift fallen men to a recognition of their kin-
ship with Christ, than to levy tribute upon the bow-
els of the earth and the illimitable caverns of the
sea, for the decoration and adornment of the home or
person, or for ministering to the convenience and
comfort of men, desirable though these objects may
be ; that it is better for a people to be rich in faith,
than in public lands, in piety than in cotton and corn,
in love than in a mercantile marine ; that duty is
more imperative than pleasure ; that to die for one's
country is better than to save life by basely deserting her in her hour of need. Of men and women
holding this persuasion firmly, and making their
practice illustrate and enforce their persuasion, the
country has most sore need. They are the salt
which will preserve us from decay. The ship of
state has by no means outridden its perils ; but is yet
environed and beleaguered by them. These perils are
not so much material as moral. If the nation does
not become bankrupt in character, it will not be
likely to become bankrupt in fortune. If it does become bankrupt in character, its gold will be a mill-
stone about its neck.

The most effectual and, indeed, the only sure, guarantee of character is love to God. Pure religion,
possessing the heart, makes a man not only a safe
element in society, but a source of security. As her
citizens become truly religious, therefore, a State
takes a new lease of life. A religion, however, which
God does not inspire, is either a delusion or a sham ;
and is, in neither case, a guarantee of character on the
part of its devotees. God, therefore, must be in the

State, and must, in some degree, inspire and guide its citizens; or a government, in which the citizens are rulers, is fatally wanting in the elements of perpetuity.

Well, indeed, might we to-day, and on other days, with ever increasing fervor, pray: "God save the Commonwealth!" God save the Republic!

NOTE.—Besides the original documents which were consulted in the preparation of this Address, the following works were employed as authorities, viz.: Judd's History of Hadley; Bancroft's History of the United States; Bradford's and Barry's Histories of Massachusetts; Holland's History of Western Massachusetts; An Address delivered at Northampton at the close of the Second Century of its settlement, by Rev. William Allen, D. D., and An Historical Address delivered in Southampton, by, Rev. Prof. B. B. Edwards, D. D.

The manuscript papers left by Col. Elisha Porter, now in custody of one of his descendants, Miss Abby P. Smith, of Hadley, to which the author was kindly allowed access, and for which he makes acknowledgment, were of important service to him. To all who in any way aided him, he also gives thanks. P. W. L.

APPENDIX.

—————•••—————

THE proclamation of the President of the United States, concerning the public observance of the Centennial Anniversary of our national independence, recommended the preparation, delivery, and preservation, of addresses, each setting forth the history of its own locality. It would, however, have been manifestly unsuitable for the author of "The History of Easthampton," in a brief address, to review the ground surveyed in that volume. He chose, rather, after sketching the period of settlement, to present an outline picture of the early part of the revolutionary struggle, giving to the picture as much of a local coloring as was possible. But, though it was needless, at present, to re-write the history of the town, it seems suitable to improve the opportunity given by the publication of the address, to bring the history down to the present time, by a brief sketch of the events of the past decade. That is the object of this appendix, which brings the survey of the town's history down to March 15, 1877.

If we look first at the religious interests of the town, we find that no change has occurred in the pastorate of the First Congregational Church. Rev. A. M. Colton is still ministering, with acceptance, to the spiritual wants of the people of that society. He is now in the twenty-fourth year of his pastorate, and is still doing good work. The deacons of the First Church are Eleazer W. Hannum, E. Alonzo Clark, and Lauren D. Lyman, the latter of whom was chosen February 3, 1870, to fill the vacancy occasioned by the death of Rev. Luther Wright. Few church officers have so long a term of service as that of Deacon Hannum, who has filled his office now for forty-three years. The relations of the First and Payson Churches are, at the present time, more than ever fraternal.

The latter is now without a pastor. For thirteen years Rev. S. T. Seelye, D. D., performed the duties of that office acceptably; but prolonged ill health recently compelled his resignation. The official relation between pastor and people was terminated January 8, 1877, in accordance with the advice of a council, of which Rev. Gordon Hall, D. D., of Northampton, was moderator, and Rev. E. G. Cobb, of Florence, scribe.

As a citizen and a neighbor, not less than as a pastor, Doctor Seelye would be missed from the community, were he to change his place of residence.

The deacons of this church are C. B. Johnson, E. H. Sawyer, M. H. Leonard, and J. H. Sawyer. The first two were serving ten years ago; and the last two were chosen December 4, 1873, and January 4, 1877, respectively. Within the period under review, A. J. Lyman has filled this office three years, but declined a re-election.

Superintendents of the First Church Sunday-school, in the past ten years, have been Lewis Clapp, Lafayette Clapp, James Keene, and J. H. Judd; and of the Payson Church School, A. B. Lyman, H. J. Bly, J. H. Sawyer, J. K. Richardson, and A. J. Lyman.

The Methodist Church, which was under the pastoral care of Rev. Franklin Furber in 1866, has since enjoyed the ministrations of Revs. C. T. Johnson, W. W. Colburn, A. J. Hall, S. O. Dyer, L. A. Bosworth, and now of E. R. Thorndike. Superintendents have been F. H. Putnam, O. H. Hill, G. A. Bullock, A. G. Dickenson, and S. W. Pierce. The society had just completed a house of worship in 1866, but was left, by the enterprise, with a burdensome debt on its hands. It has, at last, succeeded in getting the portion of this burden, which yet remains . unpaid, guaranteed by individual members of the society, and of other churches in the place.

Measures looking to the establishment of an Episcopal Church were instituted in 1871, regular services being commenced in that year, under the charge of Rev. B. F. Cooley, as a resident missionary. St. Philip's Parish was organized April 10, 1871, twenty voters of the town being chosen associates. In March, 1872, Mr. Cooley resigned, and next month, Rev. Lewis Green, then and now of Ashfield, took his place. In April, 1872, the record showed fifty-six families, forty-nine communicants, and from eighty to one hundred at the Sunday services. Mr. Green

resigned in the Spring of 1873, whereupon services were suspended until Autumn. Then the work of the parish was resumed,
and has since continued, under the direction of Rev. J. Sturgis
Pearce, Rector of St. John's Church, Northampton. Since that
time, a Sunday afternoon service has been held in the Lower
Town Hall. The society has secured a desirable site, and is preparing to soon erect a modest chapel for its use. The wardens
are N. W. Farrar and James Butterworth, the first of whom is
superintendent of a Sabbath-school numbering thirty-five children. Maj. H. E. Alvord is parish clerk.

Before leaving the religious for the secular, mention ought to be
made of the recent death, at the age of seventy, of Rev. William
Bement, the second minister of our place, and the last who was,
during his entire ministry here, pastor of the whole people.
From October 16, 1833, to April 1, 1850, he labored here with
great zeal and wisdom, and with eminent success; and became
greatly endeared to his people, whom, in turn, he regarded with
an abiding affection quite remarkable for its intensity—an affection which separation never quenched. He left here to accept a
call to the church in Elmira, N. Y., to which now, for many
years, Rev. Thomas K. Beecher has been ministering. In Elmira, he "at once commanded the highest respect of the entire
community, as a well trained, sound, scriptural preacher of the
Gospel; and as a faithful, attentive, and most acceptable pastor."

He felt parish and pulpit responsibilities with unusual keen-
ness; and, in consequence, under his arduous duties, his health
so far gave way as to compel resignation of his charge, after four
years' service. After rest, however, he was, for some five years,
minister to the Southport Presbyterian Church, where he did a
valuable work. Afterwards, for a while, he was superintendent
of schools in Elmira, and Secretary of the Board of Education.
"To this work he brought excellent scholarship, sound judgment,
and unwearying industry." Finally his health gave way, and he
suffered periods of great mental depression.

In the hope to counteract these evils, he removed to Jersey City,
where he engaged in business. His overwrought brain, however,
still gave him occasional trouble, and, early in August last—it is
supposed in a paroxysm of pain—he left his home and wandered
to the upper part of New York City, to the grounds of the Con-
vent of the Sacred Heart. Here, all alone with God, like Moses
upon Mount Nebo, he died. Days afterwards the lifeless body

was found by the sisters, the head resting upon the hand. Thus a noble life came to an end; and it matters now but little to him, that he died unattended and alone. No doubt angels were in waiting, to convoy him to the home of the ransomed. His body received burial in Elmira. His name will be long held in honored remembrance among the people of his first love.

The mention of death is a reminder that the last decade has closed the mortal career of quite a number of our fellow citizens. Though all were missed from their accustomed circles, none of them left so great a vacancy as that occasioned by the death of Hon. Samuel Williston; of whom simple justice requires that it should be said, that he contributed, very largely, to make Easthampton what it is to-day. The story of his life needs not here to be told. It is "known and read of all men." It has been in part told in previous sketches of the history of the town and seminary, in sundry other published sketches, and more fully in Prof. Tyler's admirable commemorative discourse.

Reference will hereafter be made to his last great business enterprise. To the management of that he devoted his latest years. Far on towards the close of his long life, it was his wont to drive daily to his office, and there to spend hours in oversight of his extended operations. Little by little, however, his powers of body gave way; and the time came when he must leave his business for other hands, and leave his plans for other executors, and go to his God. A growing assurance of his acceptance with God comforted his last days; though for very many years he had looked to Christ as his Saviour. "I think I am going through safe; indeed, I think I may say I *know* I am." "If there is anything I hate it is sin; and I *know* I love the Lord Jesus Christ and his cause." These were some of his latest utterances.

He died Saturday, July 18th, 1874; and was buried Monday, July 20th, from his own house. This was filled with his relatives and distinguished strangers; while those among whom his life was led, gathered in large concourse upon the lawn about the doors and windows, in expression of their sympathy and sense of loss, and to do honor to his memory. In their midst, upon the lawn, rested the burial casket. Suitable Scripture selections were read by Rev. A. M. Colton, and a brief but touching address was made by his pastor, Rev. Dr. Seelye, who also offered prayer. Deacons of the two churches, in which he had been a deacon, acted as pall-bearers while the remains were borne to the place of burial. A commemorative discourse was delivered by Prof. W. S. Tyler, D. D., in the Payson Church, on Sunday, September 13th, the whole town uniting in the service.

By his business enterprise, Mr. Williston—not, of course, without capable associates—built a town ; established a group of permanent industries; and gave employment to thousands, year after year. In doing this, he acquired a large property; but, though he had the means, he was never guilty of lavish personal expenditure. The great bulk of his acquisitions was devoted to uses which would be of public benefit. Nor did he ambitiously allow his property to accumulate, to be divided at death; but charitably appropriated about $1,000,000 during his life time. With this he founded Williston Seminary; saved Amherst College from ruin, aiding it in repeated instances; and gave largely to Iowa College, Mount Holyoke Female Seminary, and the Syrian Protestant College at Beirut.

Though his fortune was especially devoted to educational uses, religion was, in his mind, always associated with education; and that he never forgot the church, is proven by numerous gifts for religious purposes, both at home and abroad. The same devotion to public interests characterized his final division of his estate. Though he provided amply for the wants of those whom he had taken to his heart, yet the greater portion of his property was still consecrated to learning. At his death, his estate, less his debts, was valued at about $800,000. Of this sum he gave, by will, to Mrs. Williston $110,000; to his adopted children, $125,000; to numerous friends and benevolent institutions, $56,000; to Iowa College, $20,000; and to Williston Seminary, $400,000; leaving the balance, if any remained, to Amherst College. His heart was set upon a generous gift to the latter, but as so much of his estate was manufacturing property, it is feared that nothing will remain for it.

The homestead given to Mrs. Williston, and valued at $50,000, she has given to Williston Seminary, after her decease, provided at least one of the permanent buildings is placed upon the grounds, and the whole is kept for the use of the seminary.

With Mr. Williston were associated, in his early life, Revs. Luther Wright and Solomon Lyman, then young men looking forward, like himself, to professional life ; but not like him destined to be thwarted in their designs. Mr. Williston was the last of the three to pass away, though the same decade closed the life of all,

9

in their native town.   Mr. Wright had the privilege, after teach-
ing successfully elsewhere, of aiding his friend in the establishment of the seminary ; being its first principal, and holding that
position some eight years.   For many years after that, he taught
a private classical school here.   Mr. Lyman, after a useful and
earnest life work in several pastorates, came to his native place
to spend his remaining days.   These two were associated with
the church of their fathers, Mr. Wright as a deacon, and were
valued helpers there.   Other citizens, whose deaths have occurred
in this decade, are the writer's father, Daniel F. Lyman, a friend
of all these, though younger, a staunch and true man every way,
an earnest worker in the church; Capt. Ebenezer Ferry, for a
long time one of the three storekeepers here, for twenty years
postmaster, for twenty-one years town clerk, well known by all
town people and by many successive classes of students; Samuel
Wright, an old time schoolmaster of repute, one of the early town
clerks and school committee men of the town; L. Pyncheon Lyman, a thriving business man in the line of lumber and grain,
who held some public trusts; John H. Wells, for many years a
principal merchant of the town; George S. Clark, until his death
accountant of the Nashawannuck Company and influential in
town affairs; Lucas W. Hannum, who returned to his native
place late in life, and entered into its affairs with much interest;
Sidney Ferry, Capt. Luke and Lowell Janes, Joel Parsons, Augustus Clapp, Dwight and Dennis Lyman, and Zenas, Theodore
and Gilbert A. Clark,—all these, representatives of ancient families of the town, sons of sires honorably associated with its past,
and themselves bearing their lot in their day and generation, some
of them in their time filling important public station either in
town or church.   These, and perhaps others whose names do not
occur to the writer, have passed from participation in human
affairs, to the awards of the future life.   And we who remain are
each awaiting our turn.

    One who passed away not long before the opening of the decade
now in review, was Ezekiel White, a man not equaled in the
county, except by Sylvester Judd, as an antiquarian.   His library
was scattered by public auction, some of it, however, falling into
appreciative hands.   His volumes were largely freighted, upon
their margins and by inserted slips of paper, with valuable historical and genealogical notes, in his beautiful hand.   It would
be well worth the effort of the Museum Committee, if they could

secure custody of any of his manuscripts which have not been scattered.

Among those who have taken up their residence elsewhere, perhaps no one will be more greatly missed than Seth Warner. He was thoroughly identified with the town's manufacturing growth; a public spirited and influential citizen; a long time and valued church officer; and a musical expert whose leadership has wrought most excellent results.

WILLISTON SEMINARY.

Williston Seminary, which, more than anything else, makes our town known throughout the land, is prosperous as of yore; and, with enlarged scope and increased endowments, is planning for a future of even greater than her past degree of usefulness. Ten years ago, North Hall, the dormitory occupying the former site of the First Church, was approaching completion. An astronomical observatory has since been built. The grounds on the street fronts have been enclosed with a substantial and tasteful iron fence, and fronted with a sidewalk of flagging.

During the administration of Rev. Dr. Henshaw, which closed with his resignation of the office of principal at the end of the last school year, the institution has enjoyed a high degree of prosperity. Its progress has been, especially, in the enlarged facilities it has offered for the acquisition of an English education. The scientific department has been reorganized, and given increased dignity as compared with the classical.

One of the memorable events which fell within Principal Henshaw's administration, was the celebration of the Quarter Centennial, which was held on Anniversary week, July 2, 1867. There was a large attendance of graduates and former pupils. Rev. R. S. Storrs, D. D., of Brooklyn, a former teacher, was appointed President of the day. The literary exercises of the occasion took place in the Payson Church, whither the alumni repaired after an address of welcome by the Principal. A historical address was delivered by Prof. William S. Tyler, D. D., of Amherst College, the adviser and trusted friend of the founder, during the whole history of the institution. Rev. N. Adams, D. D., of Boston, in prayer, dedicated the completed buildings to the promotion of learning and religion. An oration was pronounced by Prof. Cyrus Northrop, of Yale College. Dinner had been spread in the M. E. Church, and was eaten with a relish.

At its close, the audience listened, with great interest, to an address from the President of the day, who was followed by Presidents Woolsey of Yale, and Stearns of Amherst, Revs. Luther Wright, and Josiah Clark, former Principals, Prof. Northrop, Gen. F. A. Walker, and others. The exercises of the memorable day were brought to a close by the reading of a poem, by C. H. Sweetser, Esq., of New York.

This gathering of alumni left, as its legacy, an incipient Alumni Association, which still lives and grows. It has done something towards the cultivation of an *esprit du corps* among graduates. It has meetings each Anniversary week, with a public address from some distinguished alumnus. Addresses have been delivered by Rev. H. Clay Trumbull, Prof. Judson Smith, Rev. H. M. Parsons, C. D. Adams, Esq., Judge William S. Shurtleff, and Col. Mason W. Tyler. On one occasion, a poem was delivered by Rev. Albert Bryant.

One of the most valuable results of this organization, has been the publication of an Alumni Record. This society urged the matter upon the trustees, who readily favored the project, appointed a co-operating committee, and voted to defray the expense. The matter was finally put into the hands of Rev. Joseph H. Sawyer, for several years a teacher in the seminary. With painstaking and great labor, and with the co-operation of various class secretaries, he succeeded, at length, in bringing out a most satisfactory record. It gives the addresses, and, in most cases, a brief sketch of the life, of trustees and teachers, and of one thousand four hundred and fifty-five male students; an index of the full number; the Roll of Honor; and a list of female teachers and students, with their present address and name. From this record, it appears that, at the time of publication in 1875, there had been connected with the seminary five thousand one hundred and sixty-six male, and one thousand and seventy-seven female students; total, six thousand two hundred and forty-three. Of these, the whole number reckoned alumni is one thousand one hundred and seventeen. Mr. Sawyer was able to report more or less fully concerning two thousand four hundred and ninety-four persons. Of these, five hundred and twelve had already received a college education, two hundred and five at Yale, one hundred and sixty-two at Amherst, and seventy-eight at Williams. Seventy-two were then in college. Eighty-eight more had graduated at professional or scientific schools. Of these, one hundred and sixty-seven had chosen the clerical, one hundred and seventy-four the legal, and eighty the medical professions; while seventy-seven were teachers, fifteen journalists, and twenty-five civil engineers. The Roll of Honor shows nine generals, sixteen colonels, fourteen majors, thirteen chaplains, twenty-seven surgeons, thirty-six captains, forty-one lieutenants, and two hundred and thirty non-commissioned officers and privates. Of these, forty-nine died in battle, or from exposure.

In 1873, the seminary held property which was rated at $270,000. In addition, the founder, by his will, left it a munificent endowment. Upon the settlement of the estate, it is to receive $200,000. In a few years thereafter, $100,000 more; and ultimately, $300,000 additional.

Mr. Williston's purpose was to establish neither a college, nor a professional school; but a secondary institution far superior to any now existing. To this end, the departments are to be divided into distinct professorships, to be filled by men of ability, scholarly culture, and of experience in instruction, whose duties are not to be so arduous as to prevent, and whose compensation shall be sufficient to allow, special study and research by each in his own department.

It is intended that the classical department shall not only give a most thorough fit for college; but also afford sound basis for immediate professional study, if the pupil chooses. Thorough instruction will be given in the common English branches; and also in the modern languages, with reference both to reading and conversation therein. "In the scientific department, young men are to be instructed in all the branches of science, literature, and philosophy, of a college course; and also in business forms and methods, in drawing and designing, and in architecture."

The vacancy, occasioned by the resignation of Principal Henshaw, has been filled by the appointment of Rev. James M. Whiton, Ph. D., a classical instructor of high repute, who was taken from the pastoral office in Lynn. Into his hands, with that of an able corps of associates, under the supervision of the trustees, will be committed the realization of the ideals of the founder. A part of the old board of teachers has been retained for the new administration, and other able men have been associated with them. In addition to the principal, who instructs in Latin, the faculty at present consists of the following persons, who give instruction in the branches subjoined to their names:

Robert P. Keep, Ph. D., Greek; Charles F. Eastman, M. A., Latin and Greek; Roswell Parish, M. A., Physics; Russell M. Wright, M. A., Natural History; Joseph H. Sawyer, M. A., Mental Science and History; Maj. Henry E. Alvord, C. E., Gymnastics and Engineering; Charles A. Lador, M. A., Modern Languages; George Y. Washburn, B. A., Elocution.

BUSINESS.

When the "History of Easthampton" was published, Mr. Williston had shortly before undertaken the greatest business enterprise of his life. The manufacture of cotton yarns had resulted so favorably as to encourage a great enlargement of the business; and he was, at that time, vigorously pushing to completion a mill, with a capacity of 20,000 spindles—twice that of the first mill. It was to be run by steam—a Corliss engine of 240 horse power. A corporation was formed with the title, "The Williston Mills," which had a paid up capital of $700,000. For a time at least it employed from 400 to 500 persons, with a pay roll of $9,000, and a sales account of $50,000 to $60,000 per month, and owned a village of 160 tenements (mostly only two under one roof), a store and a large boarding-house. To this enterprise Mr. Williston, who was the principal owner, gave the last years of his life, relinquishing to the hands of others the management of the industries of the upper village, in which he still retained his interest. His attempt in the new factory was to establish the manufacture of all grades of spool cotton for hand and machine sewing. With great energy and will he persevered in his undertaking, and, for several years, turned out thread in large quantities. But the competition was so sharp, and the difficulties and embarrassments of the work and of the times were so great, that the enterprise failed to be remunerative ; and, indeed, was prosecuted at so heavy a loss as greatly to cripple Mr. Williston, and sadly to disappoint his hopes as to the amount of money he was able to leave behind him for educational purposes, although, as it was, his bequests were princely.

At last he abandoned the manufacture of thread, and confined his efforts to the manufacture of cotton yarns. In this there has been better success. On account of the shrinkage of values, and the ill success of the undertaking, the capital of the corporation was reduced to $350,000 where it now stands.

The other manufacturing corporations have continued their business with varying, but on the whole with gratifying success. They have suffered at least no more than their share in the depression of the times, and have not been compelled to curtail operations to any disastrous extent.

The oldest concern, the National Button Company, has enlarged its capacity fully 50 per cent. in ten years, the mills being now capable of turning out 2,000 gross daily. In its business it employs a quarter of a million or more, though its nominal capital is but $150,000. Its President is its long-time manager, Hon. H. G. Knight, and its Secretary, H. L. Clark.

The Nashawannuck Manufacturing Company has a capital of $300,000, and a capacity of 4,000 dozen pairs of suspenders a week. Its officers are Christopher Meyer, President; Hon. E. H. Sawyer, Treasurer; G. H. Leonard, Superintendent.

The Glendale Elastic Fabrics Company has a capital of $100,000, though it employs twice that, and annually turns out products to the value of $250,000 to $300,000. E. H. Sawyer, President; M. H. Leonard, Secretary.

The Easthampton Rubber Thread Company met with a severe reverse in the burning of their mill on the night of July 12, 1869, at a loss of $135,000, with an insurance of $70,000. A new mill was, however, ready for operation in five months. It is as capacious as the old one, though with one less story. The company employ a capital of $150,000, consume in manufactures from 200,000 to 250,000 pounds of pure rubber per year, and do an annual business of from $200,000 to $250,000. H. G. Knight, President; E. T. Sawyer, Secretary and Treasurer.

The Easthampton Gas Company does a thriving business with $25,000 capital, making two and a half million feet of gas yearly. Officers are E. T. Sawyer, President; H. L. Clark, Treasurer; C. B. Johnson, Clerk.

The Valley Machine Company was formed in 1870. It succeeded the Easthampton Steam Pump and Engine Company, (of which Mr. Williston, James Sutherland and Dr. J. W. Winslow were the members.) It also purchased the business of the Nashawannuck Company's machine shop. The pump which the earlier company was making not proving a success, a new one was taken up, which is succeeding admirably. It is Wright's Bucket Plunger, patented by William Wright of New York, though greatly improved by the present manufacturers, who claim that it is now "the most simple, compact, and reliable steam pump ever offered to the public." At the Fair of the American Institute in New York, in 1870, it was rated superior to all contestants in order of merit, being considered "as effective as the best of the four valve double-acting pumps, with the advantage of having but two water valves, instead of four, to keep in order or cause trouble." The company at first received a charter, but surrendered it in 1873, and organized on a partnership basis with John Mayher as Treasurer and General Manager. A capital of $30,000 is employed. The pump has had good sale and given great satisfaction. The company propose soon to erect a foundry.

In November, 1866, J. L. Bassett bought the sawmill property on Manhan river, for many years owned by L. P. Lyman, and began the manufacture of spools and bobbins, supplying the Williston Mills with these articles. After being burned out in 1868, he rebuilt, and then went into the manufacture of thread, in which he has ever since continued. The business is conducted by a corporation, organized September, 1873, and styled "The Mt. Tom Thread Company," with a capital of $55,000. J. L. Bassett is President, and J. I. Bassett Secretary and Treasurer. About thirty hands are employed, and a business of $65,000 to $75,000 a year is done. They buy yarn, which is mostly imported, and dye, twist, and spool it. It is an excellent thread, mostly for machine use, put up in two ounce spools, and it goes chiefly to the clothing and shoe trade.

The National Button Company, the Nashawannuck, the Glendale, the Rubber Thread and the Valley Machine, each made an exhibit of their goods at the Centennial Exposition, and each received a medal as a testimonial of the excellence of their products.

Other institutions connected with the business of the place, are the First National Bank and the Easthampton Savings Bank. The former was organized in 1864, with a capital of $150,000, which has been increased to $200,000. Hon. H. G. Knight is president, and C. E. Williams cashier. An efficient board of directors co-operate in the management. Dividends have averaged 9 per cent. per annum. A surplus of $40,000 has accumulated. In its whole history, the bank has lost only $125, which is a fact without a parallel in the State. Some five years since a bank building was erected at a cost of about $20,000, which is a model structure for a country bank, being most tasteful and convenient, and having a very solidly built vault.

The Savings Bank, which was organized June 7, 1870, finds quarters in the same apartment. Cashier Williams is its Treasurer, and Hon. E. H. Sawyer President. It already has a deposit account of $182,721, three-quarters of which belongs to the townspeople. Besides its annual dividend of six per cent., it has paid three or four extra dividends.

There is no space to speak at length of the persons engaged in the trades and mercantile business of the town. Ten years have brought extensive changes; though, of those who were chronicled in 1866, as doing our mercantile business, L. Preston, A. J. Lyman, F. H. Putnum, J. E. Lambie and C. S. Rust, are still thus engaged. Of the tradesmen who were then active and are so still, E. R. Bosworth does the building, T. J. Pomeroy the undertaking, G. L. Manchester the steam and gas fitting, O. N. Clark and Wm. J. Lyman the carriage work, Wm. E. Topliff and L. G. Fales the mason work. Franklin Strong, at Loudville, still grinds grain, and E. H. and A. S. Ludden still have to do with marketing, H. F. Knapp with livery, while C. W. Langdon, then a merchant, has gone to flouring, and L. O. Toogood, then a painter, now sells fruits, vegetables, etc.

In 1686–7, Northampton gave Samuel Bartlett liberty to set up a corn-mill "on the falls below the cartway on the river." From the time when, shortly after, he used his liberty, to the present, the waters of the Manhan have not ceased to grind grain on that spot; and during all this time, a part or all the toll has been taken by the Bartletts, or their relatives the Clapps. One quarter of it is still owned by Edward Clapp, a great grandson of Major Jonathan, who received it from his uncle Joseph Bartlett, son of Samuel. It has been run five years by J. T. Thayer, who has owned three-quarters of it for two years, buying it of Cowles & Webster, who bought it of J. Pomeroy, who bought it of the heirs of L. P. Lyman, who owned a large share of it in 1866.

To supplement the previously published lists of town officers, it may be stated that C. B. Johnson was Town Clerk from 1865 to 1870, from which time until this spring, Lafayette Clapp has held the office, as he has that of Treasurer, since 1867. The present Town Clerk is Lafayette Clapp, Jr. The Selectmen of 1867–8–9, were S. Alvord, Q. P. Lyman, L. W. Hannum; of 1870, S. Alvord, Theo. Clark, A. S. Ludden; of 1871, G. L. Manchester, Theo. Clark, A. S. Ludden, and of five years, beginning in 1872, to the present, A. S. Ludden, J. W. Wilson, and H. T. Hannum.

10

The present board are H. J. Bly, A. S. Ludden, and A. P. Clark.

As Assessors during the last ten years, L. D. Lyman and L. S. Clark have each served five years, Q. P. Lyman four, A. B. Lyman, J. W. Wilson, H. T. Hannum, three each, S. Alvord two, and R. M. Lambie, C. A. Clark, M. L. Gaylord, Theo. Clapp and A. S. Ludden, one each. The newly elected board are M. H. Leonard, A. B. Lyman and S. Alvord.

The present board of School Committee consists of W. G. Bassett, W. H. Wright and L. S. Clark. In the last ten years Mr. Bassett has had eight years of service, James H. Lyman seven, making ten in all, M. L. Gaylord six, H. G. Knight two, thus completing nine years of consecutive service, R. M. Wright, four years, or six in all. L. S. Clark and W. H. Wright, are each on their second term of three years. Seth Warner, G. H. Leonard, and Miss E. B. Hinckley, have each had a term of three years, and Geo. S. Clark of two years. For a part of this time the town appointed a committee of six instead of three, as usual.

In this connection it may be remarked, that since the establishment of the High school in 1865, Miss S. E. Chapin has been in constant employ at its head.

The town was represented in the lower house of the Legislature in 1866 by Hon. E. H. Sawyer; in 1870 by Lucas W. Hannum; in 1874 by Wm. G. Bassett; and in 1876 and 1877 by Lafayette Clapp. Hon. E. H. Sawyer served two terms in the Senate, i. e., in 1867 and 1868. Hon. H. G. Knight has been twice in the Executive Council. At the present time he is honored with the office of Lieutenant-Governor of the Commonwealth, being on his third term.

Wm. G. Bassett was appointed Trial Justice in 1869, upon the resignation of Seth Warner. He held the office five years until 1874, when he resigned, and Lafayette Clapp was appointed to the vacancy.

Wm. G. Bassett and E. H. Sawyer are Notaries Public; Dr. J. W. Winslow is Coroner. The following have been appointed to the office of Justice of the Peace. The list may not be complete: Lafayette Clapp, H. G. Knight, E. H. Sawyer, J. H. Bardwell, C. E. Williams, W. G. Bassett, A. J. Fargo, L. D. Lyman, J. W. Winslow, M. H. Leonard, Rev. R. J. Donovan and Lafayette Clapp, Jr. J. L. Campbell still holds the office of Deputy-Sheriff, and, until recently, has been Tax Collector since 1869, at which time he succeeded E. W. Clark. His last term A. B. Lyman filled out. L. L. Wright now holds the office.

Wm. G. Bassett and A. J. Fargo are settled here in the practice of law. Drs. J. W. Winslow and F. C. Greene continue the practice of medicine, the former of whom has lately associated with himself Dr. Wm. M. Trow, who moved hither from a successful practice in Haydenville. Dr. C. R. Upson, a homeopathic physician, resides near Mt. Tom Station, practicing here and in Springfield.

J. H. Bardwell is in his sixteenth year in the post office. The total receipts of the office for the last year were $5,500. Probably 150,000 letters are now mailed here yearly. This is a money order office, both domestic and foreign. Foreign orders have been issued since 1872, and domestic since 1866, in which period about 10,750 orders have been given out. The office is now rated by the post-office department as of the second class, and, in the county, ranks next after Northampton and Amherst in importance. The salary it commands is $2,200.

Few Easthampton institutions have had a more variable history than its hotel; but in the last decade it has acquired something more of permanence, under the efficient and popular management of William Hill, formerly of the Mansion House, Northampton. The property he bought May 1, 1869, and changed the style of the hotel to the Mansion House. In 1870 he added a story to the main building, in the shape of a mansard roof, greatly improving its appearance. In 1871 he built a three-story extension in the rear, 80x40 feet. He can easily accommodate 100 guests, and has cared for 150. He has doubled the capacity of the house and more than quadrupled its business, receiving much patronage, during the summer season, from city guests. Much has been said, though not too much, in praise of Mr. Hill's excellent management. He keeps a thoroughly temperance house, being himself an ardent friend of this great reform.

From the census of 1875, it appeared that the town had a population of 3,969, which was a gain of 349 in five years, and of 1,100 in ten. The number of families is 730. The assessors reported the valuation, May 1, 1876, $2,274,449, the number of taxable polls 790, and of dwelling-houses 626. The tax levied in 1876, was $30,872, the rate being $12.25 per thousand. Of this the town received from the corporations within it $9,974, besides its share of the State corporation tax. One individual pays a tax of over $1,000, two over $300, nineteen over $100, and 426 only a poll tax. The town's highest indebtedness, $81,200, was reported February 1, 1872, the greater part of the debt being caused by the war expenses, and the building of the Town Hall. Since that time there has been a steady reduction. The total debt is now $39,719.20 ; or only .017 per cent. of the town's valuation, a proportion lower than can be shown by almost any town in the State. Deducting from the present debt the available resources of the town, the Treasurer reports a net indebtedness of only $29,828.46, which is matter for just pride, considering the many improvements which have been made at public expense.

Chief among these improvements should be mentioned the Town Hall. Its erection was voted in the fall of 1867. The building committee consisted of Seth Warner, E. H. Sawyer, H. G. Knight, L. W. Hannum, E. R. Bosworth, and L. D. Lyman. The foundation was begun in April, 1868. The corner stone was laid July 4, 1868. The building was ready for occupation by June, 1869.

One of the most notable days in the history of the town was that of its dedication, Tuesday, June 29, 1869. A large procession, led by the Haydenville Band, and under chief direction of Capt. F. A. Rust, moved through the principal streets, and escorted the orator and distinguished guests to the Hall. The soldiers of the war, under command of Capt. J. A. Loomis and Lieutenants J. H. Judd and H. H. Strong, were in attendance. The exercises at the Hall were in the following order :— After an overture by the Germania Band, Hon. H. G. Knight, of the committee of arrangements, introduced Hon. Samuel Williston, President of the day, who made a few remarks, after which a prayer of dedication was offered by Rev. A. M. Colton. The keys were presented by Seth Warner, in behalf of the building committee, to L. D. Lyman, of the committee to be in charge of the Hall. The principal feature of the occasion was the admirable address by Hon. Ensign H. Kellogg of Pittsfield. Brief remarks by Lieut. Gov. Tucker, closed the dedicatory services. The day was one of the finest, and an immense assemblage participated in the exercises. A concert was given in the evening by Miss Adelaide Phillips of Boston, and eighteen members of the Germania Band. It was a rare musical treat, and was enjoyed by fully 1,100 people. A promenade concert was also held on the following evening.

·The Hall is in the Lombard style of architecture, is of brick

laid in black mortar, and its height is relieved by bands of Portland stone. The front is especially ornate. It is very handsomely finished, both without and within. Its ground dimensions are 104 by 60 feet, exclusive of the towers. At the north corner is a tower 75 feet in height ; and at the south corner the Memorial Tower, 12 feet square and 133 feet high, which has near its summit an ornamental projecting balcony, affording a fine outlook. Upon its front, near the base, it supports a memorial tablet of white Italian marble, 12 feet in height, decorated on either side with columns of black marble. It ends at the top in a triangular block, surmounted by a cross. It bears upon its face the inscription :—
" Easthampton erects this tower, a memorial to these her sons, who died for their country, during the great rebellion." Then follow the names of the honored dead, twenty-two in number. Of these, Maj. Gen. George C. Strong was killed at Fort Wagner, S. C.; William Hickey, at Camp Bisland, La.; Daniel W. Lyman, at Port Hudson, La.; Charles Tencellent, at Olustee, Fla.; and Roland S. Williston, at Culpepper C. H., Va.; Alvin W. Clark, Oliver A. Clark, Rufus Robinson, Ezra O. Spooner, Frederick P. Stone, and Charles Rensselaer, died in Andersonville, Ga.; Clinton Bates and Charles L. Webster, at Baton Rouge, La.; Elisha C. Lyman and Henry Lyman, at Newbern, N. C.; James H. Clark, at Alexandria, Va.; Augustus M. Clapp, at Nashville, Tenn.; Daniel Kane, at Fredericksburg, Va.; Salmon H. Lyman, at Davis Island Hospital; Herbert W. Pomeroy, at Plaquemine, La.; Lewis P. Wait and Chauncey R. Hendrick, at home.

The first story of the building contains a small hall and rooms for the town officers, and for the public library, with ample corridors and stairways leading to the spacious upper hall. This is capable of seating 1,100. The entire cost of the structure was $65,000. The tablet cost $2,000. The architect was Mr. Chas. E. Parker of Boston, and the builder E. R. Bosworth. The masonry was supervised by George P. Shoales, and the painting by F. J. Gould. The elaborate frescoing was done by William Carl of Boston. A more complete description can be found in the published account of the dedicatory exercises.

While the hall was in process of erection, the Public Library Association was organized with corporate powers, Hon. E. H. Sawyer, its earnest advocate, securing the charter. The town appropriated two large rooms in the hall for its use, and has made it an annual grant of $500. Private donations have also been made, the chief of which have been $1,000 each from Mr. Williston and Mr. Sawyer, and $500 each from Christopher Meyer, John R. Ford, and James Sutherland. Thirty five persons have made themselves life members by the payment of $50 each. Any citizen of the town can consult the books freely at the library, and can withdraw them on payment of one dollar per year. There are at present 320 subscribers, besides the life members. The whole number of books is 4,995. There were drawn last year 13,918 books. This fact alone shows that it is a great public benefit. Miss Dora C. Miller has been the librarian from the outset, and her services have been invaluable. The present officers are E. H. Sawyer, President; H. G. Knight, Vice-President; W. G. Bassett, Secretary; C. E. Williams, Treasurer; Rev. S. T. Seelye, Rev. A. M. Colton, Lafayette Clapp and E. T. Sawyer, Directors.

The laws of the State empower Library Associations, if they so choose, to establish and maintain Museums. Our Association undertook the enterprise early in 1872, putting the matter into the hands of C. B. Johnson, H. N. Rust and Lafayette Clapp, who soon had it in successful progress. The two former have made extensive private collections, and on that account were especially well fitted for the duty assigned them. The Committee, to which L. D. Lyman was added on the departure of Mr. Rust, have worked with enthusiasm; and, with the co-operation of others, have been able to make a most valuable collection. The articles are displayed in the library reception room, and constitute a feature of decided interest, both to citizens and strangers. Many relics of the late war, and other rare and curious articles, have been collected. Some of these are illustrative of local history; others of antique customs, or of the habits of uncivilized people. Hon. E. H. Sawyer has been a steadfast friend of the work, giving to it some $300 at the start. He, with Mr. Rust of the Committee, Dr. Seelye and George S. Clark, have been the most exten- sive depositors. Space and time are wanting to mention the articles in detail. There are muskets, swords, knives, and other relics of the war, as, e. g., a piece of a rail from the field of An- tietam, riddled with bullets; a bust of John Brown, and one of his pikes; a case of stuffed birds, the work of David M. Strangford; a collection of sea shells; curiosities from the South Sea Islands; and other articles. Some of the articles have a local association, such as a set of table glasses, used about 1740, by Maj. Jonathan

Clapp; the bullet pouch that saved the life of Lemuel Lyman at Lake George, September 8, 1755; the deed of School Meadow, executed in 1745, by the agents of the town of Northampton, to Dea. Stephen Wright and Benjamin Lyman, ancestors of the Wrights and Lymans of the town; a musket made by Moses Chapman and carried by Nathaniel White in the Revolution; Rev. Mr. Williston's license to preach, signed by Jonathan Edwards; his corner clock, and an oil painting of him, presented by Mrs. Emily G. Williston; also an oil portrait of Rev. Wm. Bement, painted by Sylvester S. Lyman of Hartford, (a native of the town,) and in part donated by him. Besides the portraits, the walls are adorned by several fine engravings. The Museum Committee have a wide field from which to gather, and it is much to be hoped that the people will co-operate with them, by placing in their custody articles of historic value, which otherwise might be lost to the public. Also that they may be furnished with the means to obtain portraits of Hon. Samuel Williston, and of other representative men. If they could in any way secure photographic likenesses of those whose names are upon the tablet, their careful preservation would be a patriotic work.

Among the public improvements should be mentioned the laying of nearly five miles of concrete sidewalk, at an average cost of some twelve dollars per rod. Few towns are so thoroughly supplied with sidewalk as is this.

There is also a regularly organized and thoroughly equipped fire department, of which E. T. Sawyer is chief, and E. R. Bosworth and Wm. Hill, assistants. Pipes have been laid through the principal streets (in all 6,500 feet of iron pipe) with hydrants at proper intervals. There are at the upper mills no less than five pumps, each connecting with these pipes and capable of forcing water through the village. One is a Bucket Plunger steam pump of the largest size, owned by the town. There are two other steam pumps, and two rotary pumps run by water power, which are owned by the corporations. In case of fire, force can be instantly applied sufficient to lift a stream of water over any building within reach of a hydrant. The Williston Mills village is protected in the same way by a pump at each mill. Several of the corporations have trained hose companies, and there is besides in the town a hose company, a hook and ladder company, and the old Manhan engine company, all of which forces are under the command of the fire engineers.

Another noteworthy improvement is the laying out of Brookside Cemetery. As early as 1870, the cemetery committee called the attention of the town to the fact that, though there were frequent calls for burial lots, no more were available. The matter was not taken in hand till the following year, and, though a committee examined locations and prices, consulted as to plans, and reported progress from time to time, no full and definite recommendations came before the town from then till June 9, 1873. At that time they reported a preliminary survey of land bordering the pond at the upper village on its west side, and owned by Mrs. Williston, J. D. Ludden, J. P. Searl, Edson White and the heirs of Daniel Rust, 2d, and recommended the purchase of a suitable amount of land, the building of a bridge across the pond near the Nashawannuck office, and the construction of a road. The town voted to adopt the plan recommended, and provided a sum of money for the purpose. Ernest W. Bowdich of Boston, a civil and topographical engineer, made the final survey, beginning his work Oct. 27, 1873. This gentleman, with extensive acquaintance, declares that he knows no more finely located cemetery in Western Massachusetts, than is this. It has been named Brookside Cemetery, from its proximity to the water which adds greatly to its beauty. To interest the people in the enterprise, and to familiarize them with the location, a general invitation was given them to come together Nov. 5, 1873, and construct an avenue upon it. About 150 responded to the call. The cemetery, exclusive of the enclosing avenue, contains nearly twenty-nine acres. The whole number of lots laid out is 807, of which fifty-seven have been sold. There is ample room to increase the number of lots to 1,000 if desirable, and still leave spaces for decorative purposes. The prices range from $6 to $50 per lot. It is now in charge of a committee, E. H. Sawyer Chairman, Lafayette Clapp Secretary and Treasurer, and E. S. Janes Superintendent; with whom were associated in the early history of the enterprise, A. L. Clark, L. D. Lyman, Wm. N. Clapp and R. C. Dresser. The whole cost up to date is not far from $9,800.

Among Mr. Williston's bequests was one of $10,500 to the town for the improvement and care of the cemetery now in principal use. Of this sum, $6,500 was to be a permanent fund for keeping the cemetery in repair, and the balance was to be expended in constructing an iron fence along the front. A tasteful iron fence, with suitable gateways, has been set up as directed, which adds much to the beauty of the grounds. If the cemetery is ever removed, or the ground used for any other purpose, or if it is not kept in repair, the $6,500, with any interest not expended for repairs, is to revert to Williston Seminary. Mr. Williston deserves grateful remembrance for this generous bequest. A fine granite monument, one of the finest in Western Massachusetts, has recently been erected on Mr. Williston's private lot in this cemetery, at a cost of some $4,000, and the lot itself has been tastefully enclosed.

Increased railroad facilities have been furnished the town by the building of a branch from the Mt. Tom Station, on the Connecticut River railroad, to the village, to a station across the highway from the station of the New Haven and Northampton railroad. Over this branch the river road runs six trains a day each way, connecting with their principal trains, and collecting and delivering passengers at the Williston Mills, and at three flag stations in East Street.

In the fall of 1875, H. DeBill started, in connection with a job printing office, a weekly news sheet called The Easthampton Leader. The first number was issued October 14. Mr. DeBill enlarged it twice, and continued it through thirty-three numbers, when he sold it to H M. Converse, who changed its name to The Enterprise, and still continues its publication, doing along with it a job printing business.

For the sake of fostering and promoting a spirit of taste, and aiding in its public expression, a society called The Village Improvement Society, has been recently organized under favorable auspices. The Farmers' Club is as vigorous as ever, and enlivens the winter evenings by discussions and social festivities, at the houses of its members. Other organizations are the Easthampton Mutual Relief Association, designed to do a life insurance work for its members; the Ionic Lodge of Free and Accepted Masons; the Doric Chapter of the Order of the Eastern Star, a society somehow associated with masonry, and open to the mothers, wives, sisters and daughters of masons; the Humboldt Lodge, D. O. H., No. 97; the Caledonian Thistle Club, and the St. Patrick's Mutual Benevolent Society, mutual relief societies among the Germans, Scotch and Irish, respectively; a branch of the Society of the Grangers; the Young People's Literary Society; a successful Lyceum; and a Young People's Temperance organization.

11

To supplement the list of Easthampton College graduates given in the History of Easthampton, the following facts may be put on record.

The class of '67 in the Classical Department of Williston Seminary contained four Easthampton boys. Of these, Henry H. Sawyer graduated from Amherst College in 1871, since which time he has been in business; Charles H. Knight, from Williams College in 1871, and afterwards from the College of Physicians and Surgeons in New York City; Alvin E. Todd, from Yale in 1871, and afterwards from Yale Theological Seminary; Frank Warner was two years in Williams College, and afterwards studied music a year in Leipsic, Germany.

Frank E. Sawyer concluded his studies in Williston the same year with the four, and went thence to the U. S. Naval Academy at Annapolis, where he graduated in 1872.

George H. Baker graduated at Williston in 1870, and at Amherst College in 1874. A part of the time since he has been pursuing historical studies in Germany.

William B. Sawyer graduated at Williston in 1871, and at Amherst in 1875; since which time he has pursued the study of medicine in New York City.

Fred M. Leonard is now in Harvard College, and Arthur Wainwright is in Amherst.

Several of the young ladies of Easthampton have pursued advanced courses of instruction at Mount Holyoke and elsewhere during the last ten years.

Among these are Misses Eunice A. Lyman and Alice C. Parsons, who graduated at Mt. Holyoke in 1873. Misses Cordelia Ferry, Sarah G. Lyman, and Nettie C. Janes have taken partial courses there; and Misses Lizzie M. and Nellie J. Mayher and Sarah E. Lyman are at present in that institution. This list may not be complete, even as respects Mt. Holyoke; and certainly is not as respects all higher schools.

INDEX.

N. B.—The subjects treated of in the Appendix are indexed under the heading, Easthampton. The most important matters are indexed; but it would require too much space to give a full index of names.

84 INDEX.

Belchertown War Record.

In the course of the Author's preparation of the foregoing address, he had occasion to consult the records of Belchertown. These—with the aid of C. L. Washburn, Town Clerk—he found to contain many facts of interest respecting the doings of the fathers in preparation for, and in defence of, Independence. Such of these facts as he had space for, and as he judged of general interest, he embodied in the address. Other facts, which are of local interest, he has collected from the records and elsewhere; and presents in the following supplement, *which will only appear in those copies of the work, intended for sale in Belchertown, and which is no part of the work as published by authority of East-hampton.* The reader will notice, in the ensuing pages, references to those parts of the address where anything is recorded as to the action of this town. It will be well to read the parts of this supplement in connection with the address, as one reads notes in connection with the text. Thus the action of this town will be associated in the reader's mind with the general progress of the National cause. To facilitate such reading, the supplement will have references to the main work. The people of this town have reason for pride in the prompt and patriotic action of their fathers. It is to be regretted that the fathers did not leave behind a more complete record of the names, and amount of service, of those who had a personal share in the campaigns of the period. But have we done any better than they? It is worthy of present inquiry, whether *we* do not owe it to future generations to leave behind *us* some *more authentic and full record* than is now extant, as to the part borne by citizens of this town in the *late* war.

12

The committee to prevent the sale of imported goods, which was referred to on page 17, were Ephraim Clough, James Walker, Estes Howe, Benjamin Morgan, Lieut. Joseph Smith, Lieut. Nathan Kingsley, Reuben Barton, Serg. Joseph Bardwell, Israel Cowles and Aaron Phelps.

I copy the following item from one of the papers of Hon. Mark Doolittle, who was the most diligent and accomplished student of her history that Belchertown has ever had, and whose published and manuscript writings must always be, next after original documents, the best authority as to her early history. He says: " I find a vote September, 1774, when the regular forms of justice were suspended, (see page 20,) and the evils of anarchy and insubordination sorely felt, according to which the people, in public meeting assembled, affixed their signatures to the following solemn compact. ' We declare that we will take no unreasonable liberties or advantage from the suspension of the course of law; but we engage to conduct ourselves agreeable to the laws of God, of reason, and of humanity ; and we hereby engage to use all prudent, justifiable, and necessary measures, to secure and defend each other's persons and families, their lives, rights, and properties against all who shall attempt to hurt, injure, or invade them; and to secure and defend to ourselves, and our posterity, our just and constitutional rights and privileges.'" In this declaration one cannot but discern the spirit of a law-abiding, patriotic, people.

In the County Convention (referred to on page 20) held about this time, this town was represented by Col. Caleb Clark, Joseph Smith and Nathaniel Dwight. The latter was then Town Clerk, and records the fact that there were present delegates from every town in the County,—Old Hampshire,—but Charlemont. "They spent the day," says Dwight, "in considering the distressed state of the government, as the port of Boston is shut up by the King and Parliament; and eight or ten regiments stationed there upon the Common and upon the Neck, and digging trenches and fortifying them against the country ; and as a number of men-of-war are round about Boston, in order to oblige the province to acknowledge the right of Great Britain to tax North America at their pleasure." At said Congress they passed a number of resolves, among other things, "that it is the opinion of this Congress that a Provincial Congress is absolutely necessary."

Belchertown afterwards ratified the resolves of this Convention, and on Oct. 4, 1774, chose Capt. Samuel Howe to represent it in the First Provincial Congress, which met in Salem on the second Tuesday of that month, chose John Hancock president, and adjourned to Concord (see p. 21).

Jan. 16, 1775, Capt. Howe was chosen to sit in the Second Congress of the province, which was to meet in Cambridge, Feb. 1; and he was voted £7 15s. for his services in the first. Pursuant to advice of the County Convention, and of the First Congress (see p. 19,) whose doings they afterwards voted to sustain, the people of this town met at their meeting-house, Nov. 7, 1774, to organize a military company. They chose Caleb Clark, Captain, Joseph Graves, 1st Lieut., John Cowles, 2d Lieut., Elijah Dwight, Ensign, and Oliver Bridgman, Clerk. Foreseeing the evil, they had previously voted a sum of money for the purchase of a stock of ammunition, which they placed in the hands of Elijah Dwight. He was to sell it as it was needed, and replenish his stock from the proceeds of sale. Dec. 12, 1774, the town voted 10s. 8d. to Capt. Zachariah Eddy "for his horse's Journey to Providence to fetch Powder for the Town's Use."

Jan. 16, 1775, Belchertown honors the tax requisition of the first Provincial Congress. (See p. 22.) Feb. 9, 1775, appoints her first Committee of Safety, and passes a vote of support to that committee, which shows that toryism was at a discount here. (See p. 39.) The committee consisted of the following persons: Daniel Smith, Nathaniel Dwight, Joseph Bardwell, Israel Cowles, Ephraim Clough, Ebenezer Moody, Benjamin Morgan, Oliver Bridgman.

At the ensuing March meeting, a new Committee of Safety was chosen, consisting of Capt. Samuel Howe, Serg. Joseph Bardwell, Ensign Jonathan Bardwell, Lieut. Nathan Kingsley, Israel Cowles, Daniel Smith, Capt. Josiah Lyman.

Committee of 1776—Israel Cowles, Benjamin Morgan, Wm. Kentfield, Joseph Bardwell, N. Dwight, Col. Caleb Clark, Ebenezer Warner, Moses Hannum, Daniel and Joseph Smith, Dea. E. Clough, Capt. Z. Eddy, Lieut. Jos. Graves.

Committee of 1777—N. Dwight, Col. Clark, Daniel and Joseph Smith, Jacob Wilson, Capt. Josiah Lyman, John Cowles, Benj. Morgan, Lieut. Jos. Graves.

Committee of 1778—Capt. John Cowles, Lieut. James Walker, Benj. Morgan, Ephraim Clough, Moses Hannum.

Committee of 1779—Capt. Jonathan Bardwell, Capt. Josiah Lyman, Jacob Wilson.

The conflict which was precipitated at Lexington, roused the country to arms. Belchertown, Ware, Greenwich and Hardwick, speedily raised a company for Col. Danielson's regiment. (See p. 23.) Its officers were Capt. Jonathan Bardwell and Lieut. Moses Howe, both of Belchertown, and Lieut. Wm. Gilmore, of Ware.

Most of the men who went at this time from the county, it is said served eight months. The battle of Lexington hastened the meeting of Congress, who were summoned by the Executive Committee of the province. (See p. 23.) May 22, 1775, about a month after the battle, Nathaniel Dwight was chosen a member of the Provincial Congress called to meet at Watertown. The town voted "that said Nathaniel Dwight shall go armed *cap-a-pie*, as there is every day danger of an invasion by the King's troops that are now stationed at Boston, viz: about 4,000 men, and the government, Connecticut, Rhode Island, and New Hampshire, have 30,000 men that are stationed round about Boston." The town did not propose to give their representative full power, but chose Col. Howe, Joseph Bardwell, Daniel and Joseph Smith, and Nathan Kingsley, to give him instructions.

Maj. Josiah Lyman complains to the Committee of Safety. (See pp. 41 and 42.) He leads a company to Quebec. (See page 37.) His brother, Maj. Elihu Lyman, accompanies Arnold through Maine. (See p. 35.) Though a native of this town, the latter may not have been resident here at that time. He settled in Northfield, and finally in Greenfield.

Belchertown pledges herself to support a declaration of independence. (See p. 29.)

N. Dwight presides over a Convention of the Committees of Safety at Northampton, (see p. 41,) Feb. 5, 1777.

Dwight was an innholder, and Feb. 17, 1777, the Selectmen and Committee of Safety, of both of which boards he was a member, met at his house to regulate prices, according to authority mentioned p. 51. The state of things calling for the act in question is thus described by Mr. Doolittle: "The people were threatened with a scarcity of food, by reason of the monopolies which had been set on foot. British agents and speculators were doing their utmost to create a suffering scarcity, by purchasing up all the provisions within their reach, that they might exact exorbitant prices. This state of things produced great distress throughout the four New England provinces."

Here are a few items from the price list. (For others see p. 52.) Raw hides 3d. and calf skins 6d. per lb. Best yarn stockings 6s.; good sal tpork £4 12s., and beef £3 14s. a barrel. Flax, good and well dressed, 1s. a pound; good English hay 2s. per cwt.; good pine boards, £1 10s. a thousand; horse keep, 1s. a night; journey, 2d. a mile; "Shooing, tow and heal Corked all round" 6s.

March 31, 1777, Capt. Joseph Hooker certifies that Noble Bagg carried nineteen packs for Belchertown men to Danbury, Ct. This would indicate that early in the spring of 1777, at least as many as nineteen went from among us to the army. Recruits were soon wanted for the Continental army for three years service. (See p. 47.) Apr. 9, upon recommendation of a previously appointed committee of fifteen, it was voted to tax the town to pay any who would respond to the call, a bounty of £15, until the quota was full; also to give all non-commissioned officers and privates 10s. a month for all past services. "In consideration of the Great Hardship Capt. Josiah Lyman went through in the Last years Campane at Quebeck, and also that he has bin in the war ever since it began, Voted that his poll and estate be freed from being taxed in this Levie, for Raising men to go into the Continental service."

To gain an idea of the hardships in question, read the extract from Porter's diary, which begins on p. 37. Also the following, in which Porter gives an account of his journey from Whitehall to Ticonderoga, April 10, 1776. "Sun an hour high, set out with Captain Lyman and ten men, to attempt to break through the ice. Broke about fifty rods, till the ice was more than six inches thick; then gave out and returned back. About ten o'clock, Captain Lyman, with one man, set out upon the shore to reconnoiter. About two, returned, and brought word that a passage might be forced upon the shore. He with ten men, immediately set out with a batteau for that purpose. About two miles ahead met Captain Shepherd, and a number of others in a batteau to meet us. They had cut through two or three miles of ice, a considerable part of it six inches thick. The men went on the outside to cut through with axes. We got to Ticonderoga about dark. It rained for more than an hour before we got there."

In 1777 and 1778, calls for troops came repeatedly, and there is no doubt Belchertown responded; though the records of these years, after the votes given above, do not seem to enlighten us much as to enlistment. A call came June 8, 1779. (See p. 49.)

Thirteen men were required from Belchertown, for nine months' service. The town was called together. The selectmen in their warrant, contrary to custom, urge "that the people would universally meet." It was unanimously voted to pay £16 per month, in Continental bills, to any who would go at the call. The men were subsequently provided by the two militia companies without drawing upon the town treasury.

August 23, 1779, Col. Caleb Clark was chosen to represent the town in conventions at Concord and Northampton, to regulate prices. (See p. 51.) As he could not go, Capt. Jonathan Bardwell was sent to Concord.

Nov. 1, 1779, £410 were voted as bounty and mileage to soldiers about to depart.

Feb. 14, 1780. The depreciation in the currency at this time was such that £2,000 in bills were voted to Rev. Mr. Forward, whose salary on a silver basis had been £60. Shortly before, it had been ordered that certain bills made out on a silver basis should be paid in paper "24 double."

Belchertown buys beef for the army at £1 2s. per pound. (See p. 50). Over and over again we find them taking measures to meet a levy of beef. At a time when a silver dollar would buy two bushels of corn, the town paid several citizens ten dollars each, in paper, for a day's work, which also shows the depreciation of paper; for had it been equal to silver, it would have made a day's work equal to twenty bushels of corn. More than a year before this, to those who had furnished clothing for the army, (see p. 50,) the town voted pay at the rate of £2 8s. for a pair of shoes, £2 2s. 6d. for a shirt, and £1 16s. for a pair of stockings—six times the silver price.

There were repeated calls for clothing, to which this town responded; one e. g., Apr. 21, 1780, for a shirt, and a pair of shoes and stockings, for every ten males in town over sixteen years of age, and half as many blankets. The selectmen were directed to procure these. Again, in 1781, they were required to furnish a quantity of these articles.

In June, 1780, the town was called together to consider how to meet a requisition for troops which had just come, and they chose ten men to see on what terms recruits could be hired.

Three successive meetings were held, at the last of which a bounty of $1,000 in paper was voted, with $12 per month in hard money, including State pay. There is still preserved, a paper which shows that the town had to raise £8,400 to meet this demand, and it gives the names of those who hitherto had not done their share, upon whom this sum was levied. The £8,400 was in paper. The tax levy shows that at this time, Sept. 25, 1780, £1 in silver was equal to £72 paper.

Besides these men for the Continental army, three months' men had to be sent out at this time. Six months later, Dec. 25, we find the town appointing a large recruiting committee, to secure thirteen men for three years, or the war. They were finally secured by dividing those liable to military duty into thirteen classes, each class furnishing a man.

Six months later the town was divided into ten classes for the same purpose.

May 21, 1779, the town voted in favor of calling a State Convention to frame a new Constitution and Bill of Rights; and, on Aug. 9, they appointed Dea. Joseph Smith a delegate to the Convention which met in Concord, Sept. 1st. It continued, by adjournment from time to time, till March 2, 1780, at which time they submitted a Constitution for consideration by the people. After Belchertown had listened to the reading of it, they chose a committee of sixteen, Col. Howe chairman, " to make," or, I suppose, to *propose* " such alterations as they should think best." The Constitution was ratified by the people, and the first election of State officers ordered to take place on the first Monday of September. On that day Dea. Joseph Smith was chosen the first representative of this town in "the Grate and General Court." After that Col. Caleb Clark represented his town at least three successive terms. Once, it is recorded, that they chose a committee " to give the representative instructions, from time to time in the ensuing year, and that the representative shall act agreeable to the instructions." This was a frequent practice.

For purposes of drill and enlistment, the town had two militia companies, known at home as the East and West Companies. They were the 3d and 9th Co's of the 4th Hampshire regiment, of which at one time Col. Howe was in command. He was superseded by Col. Porter, of Hadley, upon the return of the latter from the army. This regiment included what is now Hampshire East. Dec. 31, 1778, Col. Porter made a return to the adjutant-general of the condition of his regiment. From this return I glean some facts of interest. The Lt. Col. was Ruggles Woodbridge, of So. Hadley, who had led a regiment at Bunker Hill. The Major was J. C. Williams, of Hadley. Of the 3d, which was our West Co., Jonathan Bardwell, Aaron Phelps and Henry Dwight were in command, and of the 9th, Elijah Dwight, James Walker and Edward Smith. All men physically capable, and not past a certain age, probably forty-five, were in the " training band." Those between this age and sixty-five, were on the "alarm list;" probably not required to train, but liable to be called out if a great emergency arose. At this time the West Co. had 64 men in the training band, and 25 on the alarm list. The numbers of the East Co. were 73 and 23. The whole regiment had a training band of 829, and an alarm list which brought the total up to 1,140. Besides these, there were at this time connected with the regiment 322 men in actual service, 193 of whom were in the Continental army, and 114 in the State militia.

Nearly all the men were on one or the other of these lists. At this time, within the bounds of this regiment, there were only 33 men between the ages of 16 and 60 not enrolled. The regiment had 753 good fire arms, 206 bayonets, 573 jack knives, 2,467 flints, 10,737 buck-shot, 14,778 bullets, 476 pounds of powder, 555 blankets, 321 canteens, 379 cartridge boxes of 15 rounds.

May 8, 1780, the town chose a committee from each company "to bring to an average the service that has been done in the war by each company." These were the committee men : West Co., Dea. Joseph Smith, Dea. Ephraim Clough, Lt. James Walker, Elijah Dwight, Capt. Isaac Stacy. East Co., Col. Howe, Reuben Barton, Asa Shumway, Jacob Wilson, Dr. Estes Howe. As a basis of computation in averaging, it was voted "that all past service be called 20s. a month, equal to rye at 3s. a bushel; " i. e., as I suppose, he who had paid 20s., or 7 bushels of rye for recruits, was credited with one month's service. The committee's report is still extant; but does not show how much of each man's credit arose from actual service, and how much from 20s. a month. The West Co., 83 men, is credited with 123 years' service, or an average of a year and a half each ; the East Co., 101 men, with 101 years, or a year each. That is, 184 men had supplied the government 206 years of military service, either in person or by money for substitutes, between the opening of the war and May 8, 1780. Of the West Co., 55 out of 83 had rendered more service than was due, the others less. Of the East Co., it was half and half. In making the average, the men who served with Maj. Josiah Lyman in Canada, were credited with double the actual number of months' service, because of the hardships they endured. The determination of the service due from each, seems to have been based on the number of polls and the estate which each represented. The following persons were those credited with the most service, either personal or by proxy. Of the numbers following each name, the first represents the months of service rendered; the second, the months due; the third, the number of polls the man represented, and hence, of course, the number he had who might help him meet his military obligations: Capt. Joel Greene, 81—12—2; Col. Caleb Clark, 72—42—3; Jacob Hanks, 62—18—4; Nathan Parsons, 59—16—2; Maj. Josiah Lyman, 50—15—1; Capt. Jonathan Bardwell, 44—20—1; Lt. Joseph Graves, 40—27—1; Israel Towne, 39—25—5; Dea. Joseph Smith, 41—25—3; Lt. James Walker, 37—22—2; Dr. Estes Howe, 36—8—1.

The following list comprises all the persons of whose personal service the town clerk or myself can find any documentary evidence:

Of the Dwights, Elijah and Pliny were in the service two weeks, after the battle of Lexington; and the former two months near the close of that year, and also at New York, in 1776, two months. Joseph Reed was out in 1777, 3 mos., 20 days.

In 1780, Wm. Kentfield was credited with a year's service rendered by his son Asaph. A pay-roll, still extant, establishes the fact that the following persons served about six months each in 1780, after July 4: James White, Samuel White, Thomas Fuller, Wm. Hannum, Reuben, Asa and Whitney Shumway, Elijah Parker, Stephen Darling, Joseph Towne, Caleb Stacy, Salmon Kentfield, Nath. Dodge, Nath. Doakes, Luther Clough, Enos Smith, Joel Greene, Eb. Chapman, Elijah Walker. In a paper which is extant, the Secretary of State certifies to the enlistment of four men, Samuel Pollesey, Benj. Burden, Zeph. Sturtevant, and John Hamblen, towards Belchertown's quota of three years' men, called for, March, 1782. To these must be added Capt. Jonathan Bardwell and Lt. Moses Howe, who led a Militia Co. to Boston, after Lexington; Maj. Elihu Lyman, a *native* of this place, at least, who was with Arnold in Maine; Maj. Josiah Lyman, who led a Company from Belchertown and vicinity to Quebec with Col. Porter, one of whom must have been Asa Smith,

13

referred to in Rev. Mr. Forwards' letter before. That another was Lt. James Walker, there is evidence from a manuscript list of service done, as given below, in which the word Quebec is written against his name, with the service of the year 1776. Porter speaks of "Pepe" Gilbert and F. Davis of this Company, who died in Canada. David Bridges served five months as a substitute for Col. Howe.

Of course these were only a small part of those who saw actual service, but the fathers left few records to enlighten us. Who served in all that long campaign, with Porter and others, which ended in the capture of Burgoyne; or with Washington about Boston, and afterward about New York and up the Hudson, or in New Jersey, we can not certainly tell. For some further conclusions on this point, see the Appendix (p. 98). Mr. Doolittle makes the statement that, of the citizens of this town, "twenty died in the service of the Revolutionary war."

A town meeting was called June 3, 1783, "to see if the town will come into the same or similar resolves with the town of Boston, agreeable to their request, with respect to the refugees returning back among us." They met and "voted that this town will at all times, as they have done, to the utmost of their power, oppose every enemy to the just rights and liberties of mankind; and that after so wicked a conspiracy against those rights and liberties by certain ingrates, most of them natives of these States, and who have been refugees and declared traitors to their country, it is the opinion of this town that they ought never to be suffered to return, but to be excluded from having lot or portion amongst us." This was the spirit of the people towards the tories. Whether the resolve applied to any of our citizens, I am unaware. It seems there were lands within our borders owned by tories; for March 22, 1779, "Pliny Dwight was chosen Agent to look after Refugee or tory lands, to see that there be no waste of it among the timber, or in any other way; and to prosecute trespass, if there is any."

A letter from Rev. Mr. Forward to Col. Porter, will illustrate the state of things referred to on p. 43, 44. It is dated Aug. 12, 1776, and says: "I have only time to beg a favor of you for Asa Smith. I mean not to exculpate him for deserting. But he is heartily sorry, and his return is voluntary. He has been so long in the woods, that he has been in this town but twenty days; and now pushes off with speed. And, sir, may I not suggest that the disasters of the army were such as were disheartening; and he, being at Chambly, and heard rumors worse perhaps than were true, and expected the worst; and that flight was the only way to preserve life; I say, may not these considerations be plead as an argument to recommend him to favor. He behaved well last year; and I doubt not will behave well again if he is received to favor. I dare say he will die, before he will turn his back again; but punishment will dishearten him. I beg therefore that he may be forgiven, and received to favor." As, in the average papers spoken of above, no mention is made of him, it may be that he did die rather than "turn his back."

At this distance in time, and with incomplete data, we can not determine exactly the relative rank of the fathers in point of influence; but the foregoing pages show who were some of the military and civic leaders. These additional facts may also be mentioned:

"During the Revolutionary period, Capt. N. Dwight and Daniel and Joseph Smith were Selectmen five years each, Israel Cowles three, Col. Clark, Col. Howe, Maj. Lyman, Dr. Estes Howe and Lt. Henry Dwight twice, and several others once. The military needs of the period demanded frequent town meetings. During this period Daniel Smith presided over seventeen town meetings, Maj. Lyman over sixteen, Joseph Smith over ten, Capt. John Cowles over eight, Dr. Howe over six, Col. Howe and Col. Clark over five, Capt. Zach. Eddy over four, and N. Dwight over three. The latter was Town Clerk by far the larger part of the time, though Elijah Dwight held that office for a while. The names of Committees of Correspondence and of other important committees are elsewhere given. In the Provincial Congress our members were Col. Howe twice, Capt. N. Dwight, Col. Clark and Dea. Joseph Smith. Dea. Smith was member of the Constitutional Convention, and of the first State Legislature, and Col. Clark of the next three Legislatures.

Dea. Smith's influence was perpetuated in his sons, three of whom, Amasa, Eli and John, were converted in a revival which visited the place soon after the close of the war, and became clergymen, in which office they spent long lives. One of them, John, attained to special eminence in his profession, during the last twelve years of his life filling the post of Professor of Sacred Literature and Theology in Bangor Theological Seminary.

APPENDIX.

AMONG the papers of the town is a series of four entitled: "A list of the service done in the present war for each year." 1775—1779. They are authenticated by the signature of Elijah Dwight, then Town Clerk, who endorses them as follows, under date of March 12, 1781: "The within Account passed by the Town as a Town Debt." Appended to the names is the number of months' and days' service rendered in each of the five years, and at the end the "value of the service with the interest." I have thought it would be of interest to the families of the town to know with what service the ancestors of each are credited, even if it can not be precisely determined how far the figures represent service personally done, and how far service paid for. The following is the list described, condensed as much as possible. After each man's name comes the number of months' "service done," and also the number of polls which he represented, if more than one. It is plain that a man with sons taxable, but under age, could, with their aid, render a given amount of service more easily than if alone. For the sake of brevity, surnames are not repeated; and, to secure against confusion, are given in italics. For explanation of the reference marks, see pp 99, 100.

Abbot, Nathan, 6; Bagg, Noble,‖ 13; *Bardwell*, Elijah, 13, John,‡ 19, Jonathan, Jr., 15—2, Joseph,† 12—2, Joseph, Jr.,* 3, Martin,† 12, Simeon,‖ 68; *Barton*, Moses, 14, Nathan, 11, Reuben,* 18; *Bartlett*, David,* 9—2, Solomon,‡ 11; *Billings*, Joseph,† 9, Benj. Jr.,‖ 24; *Blanchard*, Geo., 9; *Bliss*, Ebenezer,‖ 8, Wm.,† 19; *Bridgman*, Joseph, 21, Oliver,‖ 27; *Bridges*, Jonathan,‖ 10; *Capen*, Purches, 15; *Chapin*, Elijah,‖ 30—4, Luther,* 5; *Chapman*, Throop, 19; *Clark*, Col. Caleb,§ 72—3; *Clough*, Dea. Ephraim,‡ 28—3, Jonathan, 7; *Cowles*, Israel,‖ 14, Israel, Jr.,§ 13, Capt. John,‡ 26, John, Jr.,† 8; *Darling*, Stephen,* 9—2; *Davis*, Sam'l, 4; *Dodge*, Caleb,† 10—2; *Dwight*, Capt. Nathaniel,‡ 26, Capt. Elijah,‖ 24, Justus,* 30, Pliny,† 39, (father and three sons,) Lt. Henry,* 15; *Eddy*, Thomas,* 6; *Fairfield*, Thad.,‖ 11; *Fay*, James,‖ 3, Paul,‖ 4; *Gates*, Thomas,‖ 3; *Goodale*, Elisha,‖ 10; *Graves*, Lt. Joseph, 38, John,* 6; *Hannum*, Caleb,* 11, Q. M. Gideon,§ 25—4, Moses,§ 30—2, Phineas,* 6, Sam.,‖ 6; *Howe*, Col. Samuel,* 23, Lt. Moses,‡ 10, Dr. Estes,‡ 38, Elijah,† 11; *Hulett*, Lt. Mason,‖ 11, Thomas,‖ 8; *Kentfield*, David,‡ 26, Wm,† 9, Jonathan,‡ 11, Rufus,‖ 20, Salmou,† 7—2; *Kingsley*, Calvin,† 23—2; *Knowlton*, Roswell,† 14; *Lee*, Phineas,† 7—2; *Livermore*, Isaac, 3; *Lyman*, Maj. Josiah,§ 44; *Moody*, Ebenezer,‖ 16; *Morgan*, Benj, 16—3; *Nash*, Jonathan,‖ 3, Reuben,§ 8; *Needham*, Daniel, 3; *Newton*, Asa,† 5; *Olds*,‡ Widow —— 18; Justin, 7; *Palmer*, David, 6; *Parker*, Elijah, 11; *Parsons*, Adjt. Nathan,‡

47—2; *Phelps*, Lt. Aaron,‖ 17, Eliakim,* 17; *Pratt*, Abraiam, 2, David,† 9, Jabez, 4, James,§ 8, Micah,† 7; *Prentice*, Moses,* 11; *Ramsdell*, Joseph,† 7; *Read*, Josepi, 4; *Rice*, Timotiy, 7; *Root*, Elisia,‖ 12, Hezekiai,§ 29—2, Orlando, 8; *Ruggles*, Timotiy, 19; *Sawin*, James, 9; *Shumway*, Asa,† 8, Cyril, 4, Sergt. David,‖ 11, Levi,‖ 17, Nathan,† 15, Solomon,† 10, Stepien,‖ 4; *Sikes*, Josepi, 6; *Smith*, Lt. Daniel,‡ 21—2, Lt. Edward, 17, Hezekiai,* 14, James,* 7, Dea. Joseph,§ 26—3, Joseph, Jr., 9, Lemuel,* 13, Tiomas,* 6; *Stanley*, Abisha,* 8; *Stacy*, Capt. Isaac,‡ 27—3; *Stebbins*, Lt. Gideon,‖ 20; *Thayer*, Enoch,† 5, Noai, 8; *Thurston*, Tiomas, 7, Paul,* 12; *Torrence*, Thomas,† 10, Wm., 5; *Towne*, Israel,‖ 39—3, David,§ 19—2, Francis, 7; *Walker*, Lt. James,‖ 24—2; *Warner*, Ebenezer,‖ 12, Elisha,‡ 17, Jonathan,* 10, Josiai,‖ 7, Seth,* 30; *Ward*, Jesse, 6, John,§ 22—2, Join 3d,* 8, Obadiai, Jr.,§ 8, Samuel,‡ 8; *White*, James,* 2; *Whitney*, Benj.,§ 29—4, Benj. Jr.,* 8; *Williams*, Darling, 7, Joseph,‡ 19—3, Tiomas,‖ 12; *Wilson*, Asa, 7, Jacob,* 12, Samuel,§ 13—3, Tiomas, 8, Jacob 3d, 1.

On one of the sieets the Town Clerk adds to his endorsement as before given, " with additions to be made of tiose tiat iave not brougit in tieir account." Tiese names are on the list, but no amount of service specified; Sam. and James Blair, Simon Blanciard, Benj. Burdon, James Clark, Reuben Coates, Jona. Flynt, Nati. Goodale, Lt. M. Gray, Seti Hulett, Asa, Eben and Josiai Hill, Join Jordan, Enoci Olds, Nati. Perry, Elijai Tiayer, Elijah Turner, Eliiu Warner, and Capt. Joel Greene, who is credited in the average papers witi 81 mos. (2 polls), and who was also, at a later period, six montis at least in service, as were several otiers in the list above. Mary Wiite, Raciel Hannum, and Elizabeti Crawfoot, are named as widows to wiom the town was indebted. Periaps tieir iusbands died in the service.

It is certain tiat some of the above was iired service; for Captain Elijai Dwigit, Town Clerk, certifies tiat his fatier, Natianiel, iired a man for 8 mos., in 1775, and tiat his brotiers, Justus and Pliny, eaci iired one a year to go to Quebec; and tiis iired service is credited to tiem in the list. Moreover, in several instances, men are credited witi more months' service in a year tian the year has montis, and tiat in the case of men representing but one poll; so tiat it is certain "service done" in tiis list, includes service *hired*. Each of the Dwigit family are credited witi 18 montis' service in 1777, Josepi Graves witi 36, Moses Hannum, 18, David Kentfield, 18, Dr. E. Howe, 28, Calvin Kingsley, 19, Tim. Ruggles, 19, and Rufus Kentfield, 19; Simeon Bardwell with 55 montis in the first tiree years; Pliny Dwigit witi 20 montis in '76, and Tiroop Ciapman witi 15, Oliver Bridgman witi 19, and Col. Caleb Clark witi 60, in '78·

Capt. Elijai Dwigit, in a paper still extant, certifies tiat he and his brotier Pliny were "gon a fortnet after Lexenton figit." Twenty-one men are credited witi about tiat amount of service tiat year, most of tiem witi 15 days. Putting tiis and tiat togetier, the autior concludes tiat tiey went in person to Boston, in the first uprising, with Capt. Jonatian Bardwell and Lt. Moses Howe, who, according to Dr. Holland, led our company. The names of tiese are marked in the list witi a dagger, tius (†).

Lt. Howe is credited witi 8 montis', 15 days' service in 1775. So also are fifteen others. Is it unreasonable to conclude that tiey served witi him about Boston? Their names in the list are marked witi the double dagger, tius (‡).

14

Fourteen others are credited with *nearly* the same amount of service, that year, either more or less, w ose names bear the section mark, thus (§).

All ot ers who rendered service in 1775, are marked wit parallel lines, thus (‖). Their period of service was from one mont , upward.

Most of t ese who served in 1775 did so also in 1776 or 1777, or bot . Those w ose first service was in 1776, are marked wit a star. All in the list, wit no reference mark by their names, rendered t eir first service in 1777, with the exception of Davis, Needham, Jesse Ward and A. Pratt, who began in 1778.

Judging from w at was true in the last war, and from the fact that little is said about raising bounty money till 1778, the aut or concludes t at service credited to a man in the first years of the war, is *more likely* to ave been *actual* service t an t at credited to him in its later years, t oug it is certain t at some of the latter was actual service, and some of the former ired service. For example, N. Dwig t is credited with 8 mont s, 15 days in 1775 ; but his son Elija certifies t at it was ired. During a part of that time, he was in the Provincial Congress, "armed *cap-à-pie*," according to the instructions of his townsmen. Simeon Bardwell, also, that year, is credited with 17 months' service, t oug he represented only imself; he must t erefore ave paid for a part, at least. It is, ence, certain t at *not all* the service even of the first year, was in person, t oug a large part of it doubtless was.

The list whic has now been undergoing analysis, fails to mention the following who are credited wit more or less service in the "average papers" referred to on a previous page. Capt. Jonathan Bardwell, (who led the first company from town and is credited wit 44 mont s,) Jacob Hanks, Jo n W ite, J. Robinson, J. Mosley, Jacob Wilson, Jr., O. Ward, Jos. Williams, Jr., Jas. Hulett, Elija Fay, Wm. and Jos ua Allen, Abner Eddy, Elija Lee, Matt ew Moody, Eldad Parsons, Dr. Amasa Scott, Oliver Wrig t, Sam. Worthington, Widow Elizabet Eaton.

The papers give some reason to suppose t at, among the Canada soldiers wit Captain Lyman and Lt. James Walker, were Lt. Gideon Stebbins, Adjt. Nat an Parsons, Dea. Josep Smit and Elis a Root. As a fact of interest it may be said that t ese papers s ow t at Major Josep Hawley, of Nort -ampton, was among the non-resident land- olders ere, paying taxes on 850 acres.

The names of the twenty dead who made the greatest sacrifice, sealing t eir patriotism wit t eir lives, do not appear ere, unless some of t em died after 1781. If t eir names could be ascertained, they would deserve to stand at the ead of our list of Revolutionary eroes. No one can be better aware t an is the aut or, of the unsatisfactory state in w ic t is review leaves the question as to who of our citizens actually performed military service ; but t is is presented as the best approximation to an answer w ic considerable examination and study has enabled him to give, and he t oug t t at t ose interested in the patriotic doings of t eir fat ers, would find pleasure in an examination of the list. T oug no doubt many mout s' service were done by proxy, yet it is probable t at the greater part of t ose w ose names are given, saw actual campaigning at one time or anot er.

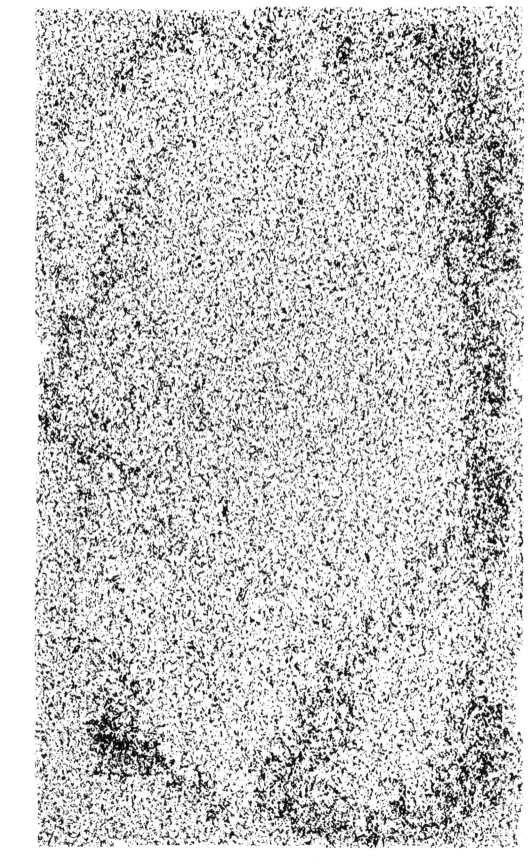

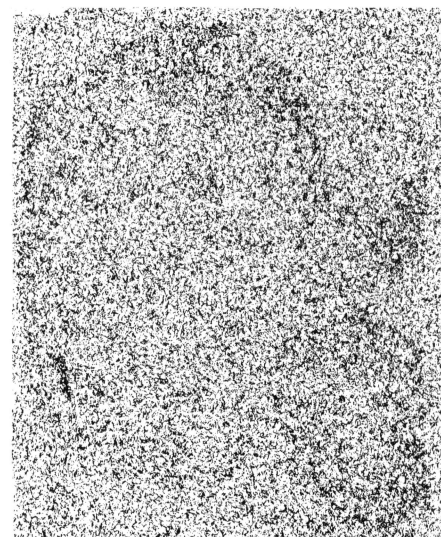

CPSIA information can be obtained
at www.ICGtesting.com
Printed in the USA
BVHW061800170119
538109BV00020B/458/P